CONTINENTS IN CLOSE-UP

EUROPE

MALCOLM PORTER and KEITH LYE

CHERRYTREE BOOKS

CONTINENTS IN CLOSE-UP
EUROPE

This illustrated atlas combines maps, pictures, flags, globes, information panels, diagrams and charts to give an overview of the whole continent, a closer look at each of its countries and at the Atlantic and Arctic oceans.

COUNTRY CLOSE-UPS

Each double-page spread has these features:

Introduction The author introduces the most important facts about the country or region.

Globes A globe on which you can see the country's or region's position in the continent and the world.

Flags Every country's flag is shown.

Information panels Every country has an information panel which gives its area, population and capital, and where possible its currency, religions, languages, main towns and government.

Pictures Important features of each country are illustrated and captioned to give a flavour of the country. You can find out about physical features, famous people, ordinary people, animals, plants, places, products and much more.

Maps Every country is shown on a clear, accurate map. To get the most out of the maps it helps to know the symbols which are shown in the key on the opposite page.

Land You can see by the colouring on the map where the land is forested, frozen or desert.

Height Relief hill shading shows where the mountain ranges are. Individual mountains are marked by a triangle.

Direction Except for the map of the Arctic, all of the maps are drawn with north at the top of the page.

Scale All of the maps are drawn to scale so that you can find the distance between places in miles or kilometres.

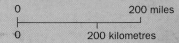

A Cherrytree Book

Designed and produced by
AS Publishing
Text by Keith Lye
Illustrated by Malcolm Porter and Raymond Turvey

First published 2001
by Cherrytree Press
327 High Street
Slough
Berkshire
SL1 1TX

Copyright © Malcolm Porter and AS Publishing

British Library Cataloguing in Publication data

Porter, Malcolm
  Europe. - (Continents in close-up)
  1.Children's atlases
  2.Europe - Maps for children
  I.Title II.Lye, Keith
  912.4

ISBN 1 842 34027 1

Printed in Hong Kong

KEY TO MAPS

FRANCE	Country name
Lapland	Region
~~	Country border
▪	More than 1 million people*
•	More than 500,000 people
·	Less than 500,000 people
☐	Country capital
ᴀLᴾˢ	Mountain range
▲ *Mont Blanc 4807m*	Mountain with its height
∴ *Stonehenge*	Archaeological site

Rhine	River
⌐⌐⌐	Canal
▬	Lake
┬	Dam
▬	Island

	Forest
	Crops
	Dry grassland
	Desert
	Tundra
	Polar

Many large cities, such as Birmingham, have metropolitan populations that are greater than the city figures. Such cities have larger dot sizes to emphasize their importance.

CONTINENT CLOSE-UPS

People and Beliefs Map of population densities; chart of percentage of population by country; chart of areas of countries; map of religions.

Climate and Vegetation Map of vegetation from polar to desert; maps of winter and summer temperatures; map of annual rainfall.

Ecology and Environment Map of environmental damage to land and sea; maps showing deaths caused by heart disease, cancers and fatal road accidents; panel of endangered animals and plants.

Economy Map of agricultural and industrial products; chart of gross national product for individual countries; panel on per capita gross national products; map of sources of energy.

Politics and History Panel of great events; map of location of major events in European history; timeline of important dates; maps of prehistoric sites, the Roman empire, 20th century conflicts and the European Community.

───────

Oceans Maps of the Atlantic and Arctic oceans, and panels of statistics.

───────

Index All the names on the maps and in the picture captions can be found in the index at the end of the book.

CONTENTS

Reindeer
see page 7

EUROPE

Europe is the sixth largest continent, covering about seven per cent of the world's land area. Only Australia is smaller. Europe was the home of several major civilizations and its culture has had a great influence on the rest of the world.

In the east, Europe borders Asia. The boundary with Asia runs along the Ural Mountains and the Ural River to the Caspian Sea and then through the Caucasus Mountains. About a quarter of Russia lies in Europe, while the rest is in Asia. Smaller parts of four other countries also lie in Europe.

European Union This is an alliance of 15 European countries that work together to create a single economy and, through friendly co-operation, promote democracy and prevent wars. The headquarters is in Brussels (above), the parliament in Strasbourg.

Napoleon I (1769-1821) was a great military leader who became emperor of France. His armies conquered an empire that covered most of central and western Europe. Europe has been the scene of many great wars.

EUROPE
Area: 10,443,000sq km
(4,032,000sq miles)
Population: 705,600,000
Number of independent countries: 4
(including European Russia, but not Azerbaijan, Georgia, Kazakhstan and Turkey, which are mainly in Asia)

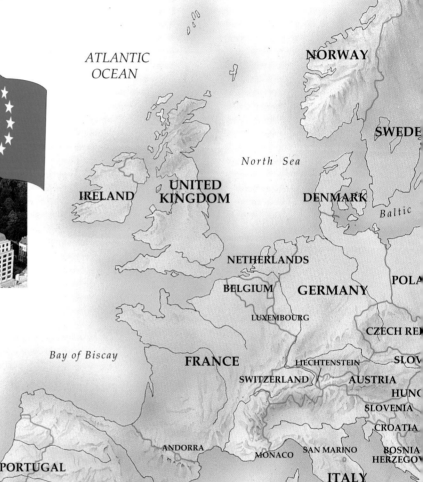

ICELAND

ATLANTIC OCEAN

NORWAY

SWEDE

North Sea

IRELAND

UNITED KINGDOM

DENMARK

Baltic

NETHERLANDS

BELGIUM

GERMANY

POLA

LUXEMBOURG

CZECH REI

Bay of Biscay

FRANCE

LIECHTENSTEIN

SLOV

SWITZERLAND

AUSTRIA

HUNG

SLOVENIA

CROATIA

ANDORRA

MONACO

SAN MARINO

BOSNIA HERZEGO

PORTUGAL

ITALY

SPAIN

VATICAN CITY

GIBRALTAR (UK)

MEDITERRANEAN SEA

MALTA

| 0 | 250 miles |
| 0 | 250 kilometres |

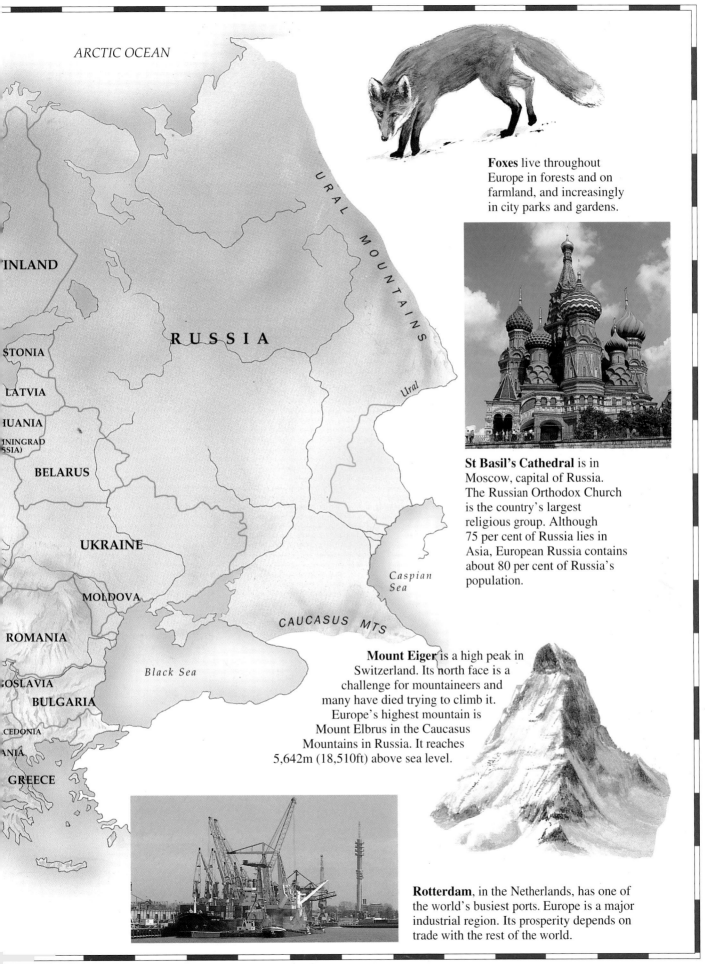

ARCTIC OCEAN

URAL MOUNTAINS

Ural

FINLAND

STONIA

LATVIA

HUANIA

NINGRAD
SSIA)

BELARUS

RUSSIA

UKRAINE

MOLDOVA

Caspian
Sea

ROMANIA

Black Sea

GOSLAVIA

BULGARIA

CEDONIA

ANIA

GREECE

CAUCASUS MTS

Foxes live throughout Europe in forests and on farmland, and increasingly in city parks and gardens.

St Basil's Cathedral is in Moscow, capital of Russia. The Russian Orthodox Church is the country's largest religious group. Although 75 per cent of Russia lies in Asia, European Russia contains about 80 per cent of Russia's population.

Mount Eiger is a high peak in Switzerland. Its north face is a challenge for mountaineers and many have died trying to climb it. Europe's highest mountain is Mount Elbrus in the Caucasus Mountains in Russia. It reaches 5,642m (18,510ft) above sea level.

Rotterdam, in the Netherlands, has one of the world's busiest ports. Europe is a major industrial region. Its prosperity depends on trade with the rest of the world.

5

NORTHERN EUROPE

Northern Europe contains Scandinavia, a region that consists of Norway and Sweden. It also includes Finland and the small country of Denmark.

   The climate is mostly unsuitable for farming, except in the south. The region's resources include Norway's oil, which it gets from the North Sea, its many rivers, which are used to produce hydroelectricity, and huge forests. Manufacturing is now the most valuable activity in all four countries.

DENMARK

Area: 43,094sq km (16,639sq miles)
Highest point: 173m (568ft)
Population: 5,284,000
Capital and largest city: Copenhagen (pop 1,346,000, including suburbs)
Other large cities: Århus (209,000)
Odense (143,000)
Ålborg (117,000)
Official language: Danish
Religions: Christianity (Lutheran 87%)
Government: Monarchy
Currency: Danish krone

FINLAND

Area: 338,145sq km (130,559sq miles)
Highest point: Mount Haltia 1,324m (4,344ft)
Population: 5,140,000
Capital and largest city: Helsinki (pop 875,000, including suburbs)
Other large cities: Tampere (186,000)
Turku (167,000)
Oulu (112,000)
Official languages: Finnish, Swedish
Religions: Christianity (Lutheran 86%)
Government: Republic
Currency: Markka, Euro

NORWAY

Area: 323,877sq km (125,050sq miles)
Highest point: Galdhøppigen 2,469m (8,100ft)
Population: 4,404,000
Capital and largest city: Oslo (pop 494,000)
Other large cities: Bergen (224,000)
Trondheim (145,000)
Stavanger (108,000)
Official language: Norwegian
Religions: Christianity (Lutheran 88%)
Government: Monarchy
Currency: Norwegian krone

Fiords are long, narrow inlets of sea that stretch along the ragged, mountainous coast of Norway. One of them, called Sogne Fiord, extends 200km (124 miles) inland.

Oil is extracted from deposits under the North Sea. Fuels and fuel products are Norway's leading exports. Farming, forestry, fishing and manufacturing are other major activities in northern Europe.

SWEDEN

Area: 449,964sq km (173,732sq miles)
Highest point: Mount Kebnekaise 2,111m (6,926ft)
Population: 8,849,000
Capital and largest city: Stockholm (pop 718,000)
Other large cities: Göteborg (454,000)
Malmö (248,000)
Official language: Swedish
Religions: Christianity (Church of Sweden 86%)
Government: Monarchy
Currency: Swedish krona

ATLANTIC OCEAN

Trondheim

Ålesund

Galdhøppigen 2469m

Bergen

NORWAY

Glåma

Stavanger

Oslo

Skien

Fredrikstad

Kristiansand

Lake Vänern

Skagerrak

Borås

Vätte

North Sea

Göteborg

Ålborg

Kattegat

Jutland

Århus

173m

DENMARK

Esbjerg

Copenhagen

Odense

Malmö

Bornho

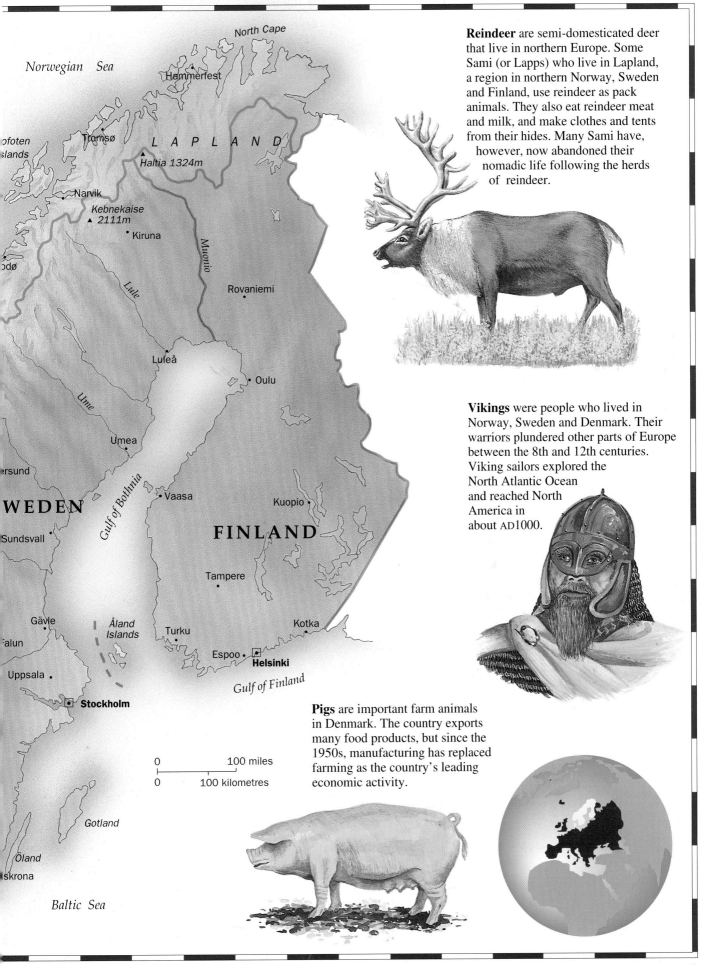

Reindeer are semi-domesticated deer that live in northern Europe. Some Sami (or Lapps) who live in Lapland, a region in northern Norway, Sweden and Finland, use reindeer as pack animals. They also eat reindeer meat and milk, and make clothes and tents from their hides. Many Sami have, however, now abandoned their nomadic life following the herds of reindeer.

Vikings were people who lived in Norway, Sweden and Denmark. Their warriors plundered other parts of Europe between the 8th and 12th centuries. Viking sailors explored the North Atlantic Ocean and reached North America in about AD1000.

Pigs are important farm animals in Denmark. The country exports many food products, but since the 1950s, manufacturing has replaced farming as the country's leading economic activity.

Norwegian Sea

North Cape

Hammerfest

L A P L A N D

Tromsø

Haltia 1324m

Lofoten Islands

Narvik

Kebnekaise ▲ 2111m

Kiruna

Muonio

Bodø

Lule

Rovaniemi

Ume

Luleå

Oulu

Umea

Gulf of Bothnia

Vaasa

Kuopio

SWEDEN

Östersund

Sundsvall

FINLAND

Tampere

Gävle

Åland Islands

Turku

Kotka

Falun

Espoo

Helsinki

Uppsala

Gulf of Finland

Stockholm

0   100 miles

0   100 kilometres

Gotland

Öland

Karlskrona

Baltic Sea

ICELAND

Iceland, in the North Atlantic Ocean, is often called the 'land of ice and fire'. Large bodies of ice cover about one-eighth of the land and the country has about 200 volcanoes. The main industry is fishing and fish processing.

 ICELAND

Area: 103,000sq km (39,769sq miles)
Highest point: Hvannadalshnúkur 2,119m (6,952ft)
Population: 271,000
Capital: Reykjavik (pop 105,000)
Official language: Icelandic
Religions: Christianity (Lutheran 90%)
Government: Republic
Currency: Icelandic krona

Geysers are hot springs that throw up high jets of steam and hot water. The water is heated by underground volcanic rocks. It is used to heat buildings and supply homes with hot tap water.

Fishing is important in the waters around Iceland. Fish and fish products account for more than seven-tenths of the country's exports. Iceland has little farmland, though some farmers keep sheep and cattle.

Isafjördhur

Siglufjördhur

Blönduos

Akureyri

Seydisfjördhur

ICELAND

Vatnajökull

Hofn

 Reykjavik
Hafnarfjördhur

▲ Hvannadalshnúkur
2119m

ATLANTIC OCEAN

Heimaey

Vik

○ Surtsey

0		50 miles
0		50 kilometres

Surtsey is a volcanic island that appeared off southern Iceland in 1963. It was named after Surt, the Norse god of fire.

8

IRELAND

Ireland consists of the Republic of Ireland, which makes up five-sixths of the island, and Northern Ireland which is part of the United Kingdom (see page 10). Farming is important in Ireland, but manufacturing and new technology and service industries are the most valuable activities.

IRELAND

Area: 70,284sq km (27,137sq miles)
Highest point: Carrauntoohill 1,041m (3,141ft)
Population: 3,661,000
Capital and largest city: Dublin (pop 481,000)
Other large cities: Cork (127,000)
Official languages: Irish, English
Religions: Christianity (Roman Catholic 92%)
Government: Republic
Currency: Irish pound, Euro

Giant's Causeway is probably Northern Ireland's best-known tourist attraction. It was formed when molten lava cooled to form masses of six-sided columns made of a rock called basalt.

Shamrock is Ireland's national symbol. It is a kind of clover that, according to legend, St Patrick planted. Its three leaves represent the Holy Trinity.

Giant's Causeway

Coleraine

Londonderry

NORTHERN IRELAND

Antrim

Bann

Omagh

Lough Neagh

Belfast

Lower Lough Erne

Lurgan

Portadown

Upper Lough Erne

Newry

Sligo

Dundalk

Lough Conn

Carrick-on-Shannon

Lough Mask

IRELAND

Drogheda

IRISH SEA

Lough Ree

Lough Corrib

Athlone

Galway

Shannon

Liffey

Dublin

Galway Bay

Roscrea

Lough Derg

Wicklow

Barrow

Limerick

ATLANTIC OCEAN

Clonmel

Tralee

Wexford

Waterford

Killarney

Carrauntoohill 1041m

Lee

Cork

| 0 | | 50 miles |
| 0 | | 50 kilometres |

Potatoes, barley, sugar beet and wheat are leading crops in Ireland. Cattle and dairy products, pigs and sheep are important farm animals.

Celtic crosses and other carved stone monuments are found throughout Ireland.

9

UNITED KINGDOM

The United Kingdom of Great Britain and Northern Ireland (often called the UK, or Britain) includes England, Scotland and Wales, which are together called Great Britain, and Northern Ireland (see map on page 9).

The Industrial Revolution began in England in the late 18th century and today the country plays a major part in world trade. It is the most densely populated country in Europe.

UNITED KINGDOM

Area: 243,305sq km (93,941sq miles)
Highest point: Ben Nevis 1,343m (4,406ft)
Population: 59,200,000
Capital and largest city: London (pop 7,074,000)
Other large cities: Birmingham (1,020,000)
Leeds (727,000)
Official language: English
Religions: Christianity (66%)
Government: Monarchy
Currency: Pound sterling

ENGLAND
Area: 130,395sq km (50,346sq miles)
Population: 49,500,000
Capital: London (pop 7,074,000)

NORTHERN IRELAND
Area: 13,843sq km (5,345sq miles)
Population: 1,700,000
Capital: Belfast (pop 284,000)

SCOTLAND
Area: 78,313sq km (30,237sq miles)
Population: 5,100,000
Capital: Edinburgh (pop 450,000)

WALES
Area: 20,754sq km (8,013sq miles)
Population: 2,900,000
Capital: Cardiff (pop 321,000)

ISLE OF MAN & CHANNEL ISLANDS
The Isle of Man in the Irish Sea and the Channel Islands off the coast of northwest France are British dependencies, but they are not part of the United Kingdom.

William Shakespeare (1564-1616) is widely regarded as the world's greatest poet and dramatist. Britain has also produced many other celebrated writers, and the language in which they have written is now spoken in many countries.

Stonehenge is an ancient monument in southern England. It is a circle of huge stones that were probably used for religious purposes. It was built between about 2800 and 1500 BC.

Sheep are raised in highland areas, cattle and pigs on lowland farms. Agriculture is important but the country imports food. Most of its wealth comes from manufacturing, trade and services such as banking, insurance, finance and tourism.

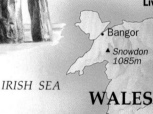

John o' Groats
W
Lewis
Hebrides
North West Highlands
Skye
Inverness
Loch Ness
Spey
Grampian
Fort William
Ben Nevis 1343m
Dun
Perth
Loch Lomond
SCOTLAND
Glasgow Clyde **Edinb**
Ayr
Dumfries
Ca
Isle of Man
Scafel 978m
Douglas
Blackp
Liverp
Bangor
Snowdon 1085m
IRISH SEA
WALES
Aberystwyth
Swansea
N
Cardiff
B
Exeter
Plymouth
Penzance
Land's End
Isles of Scilly

Orkney
Islands

•Wick

Shetland
Islands

Lerwick

een

Golf developed in Scotland, where the first organized golf club was set up in 1744. Soccer is, however, by far the most popular sport in the United Kingdom.

NORTH SEA

ick-upon-Tweed

wcastle upon Tyne

•Sunderland

•Middlesbrough

York

Bradford

Leeds

Kingston upon Hull

hester

• Sheffield

n-Trent _Trent_

•Nottingham

NGLAND

Norwich

• Leicester

erhampton

•Coventry

ngham

Cambridge

Northampton

• Ipswich

Oxford

• Luton

Thames ■

London

Reading

nehenge

Dover

Southampton

Portsmouth

Brighton

emouth

Isle of Wight

English Channel

Channel Islands

Guernsey

FRANCE

Jersey

London Eye Built by the River Thames to mark the millennium, this is the largest observation wheel in the world. From the top you can see for 40km (25 miles).

Puffins are sea birds found mostly on the north and west coasts of Britain. The country has many animal species, though numbers have declined because of human population pressures and pollution.

London was founded by the Romans in AD 43 on the River Thames. It has many historic buildings. The business heart of London, called the City of London, is an internationally important financial centre.

0	50 miles
0	50 kilometres

LOW COUNTRIES

The Low Countries lie at the western end of a huge plain that extends across Europe from the North Sea to the Ural Mountains in Russia. Much of the land is flat. Large areas, especially in the Netherlands, were once under the sea. They would still be flooded if the Dutch had not built dikes (strong sea walls). Farming is important in this region, but manufacturing is the most valuable activity.

BELGIUM

Area: 30,519sq km (11,783sq miles)
Highest point: Botrange Mountain 694m (2,277ft)
Population: 10,190,000
Capital and largest city: Brussels (pop 948,000)
Other large cities: Antwerp (456,000)
Ghent (226,000)
Official languages: Dutch, French, German
Religions: Christianity (Roman Catholic 88%)
Government: Federal monarchy
Currency: Belgian franc, Euro

LUXEMBOURG

Area: 2,586sq km (998sq miles)
Highest point: Buurgplatz 559m (1,835ft)
Population: 422,000
Capital: Luxembourg (pop 76,000)
Languages: Luxemburgian, French, German
Religions: Christianity (Roman Catholic 95%)
Government: Monarchy (Grand Duchy)
Currency: Luxembourg franc, Euro

NETHERLANDS

Area: 40,844sq km (15,770sq miles)
Highest point: 321m (1,053ft)
Population: 15,607,000
Capital and largest city: Amsterdam
(pop 718,000)
Other large cities: Rotterdam (593,000)
The Hague (442,000)
Official language: Dutch
Religions: Christianity (Roman Catholic 32%, Dutch Reform Church 15%, Calvinist 8%)
Government: Monarchy
Currency: Guilder, Euro

0   50
0   50 kilometres

NORTH SEA

Haarlem
Amste
Leide
The Hague
Delft
Rotter

Windmills have been used for centuries to operate pumps to drain water from flat land in the Low Countries. Farming is a major activity. Flowers and bulbs are well-known products of the Netherlands.

Ostend
Bruges
Ghent
Scheldt
Antwerp
Mechelen
Kortrijk
■ Brussels

BELGIUM

Mons

Charleroi

Brussels has a fine city centre and is an international meeting place. It is in a bilingual (two-language) region of Belgium, where both Dutch and French are spoken. Other regions include the Dutch-speaking Flemish Region in the north and the French-speaking Walloon Region in the south.

NETHERLANDS

sian Islands

Leeuwarden

Groningen

selmeer

Zwolle

IJssel

Almelo

Apeldoorn

Enschede

Rhine

Arnhem

Nijmegen

ertogenbosch

Maas

Eindhoven

Genk

Heerlen

Maastricht *321m*

Liège

Botrange ▲
694m

d e n n e s

▲
Buurgplatz 559m

LUXEMBOURG

Luxembourg
▣

Esch-sur-Alzette

Barges are used to transport goods along rivers and canals. Rotterdam in the Netherlands and Antwerp in Belgium are among the world's busiest ports.

Computers and electronic products are important in the Netherlands. The country also produces many other technically advanced goods. Belgium is famous for its ancient textile industry, while Luxembourg is a major steel producer.

Bicycles and motorcycles are popular means of transport across the flat countryside. The Low Countries have a good network of paved roads and most families own a car.

Grand Ducal Palace This is the home of the Grand Duke (or Duchess) of Luxembourg, the country's head of state. Though the countries are all democracies, the Low Countries have a long monarchist tradition.

GERMANY

In 1945, at the end of World War II, Germany was in ruins. From 1949, it was divided into two parts. West Germany, with aid from western countries including the United States, recovered quickly from the war. It soon became a prosperous industrial democracy. East Germany, under a Communist government, was much less prosperous. The two Germanies were reunited in 1990. This was the first of several major changes to the map of Europe that occurred during the 1990s.

GERMANY

Area: 356,980sq km (137,831sq miles)
Highest point: Zugspitze, near the Austrian border, 2,963m (9,721ft)
Population: 82,071,000
Capital and largest city: Berlin (pop 3,470,000)
Other large cities: Hamburg (1,707,000)
Munich (1,240,000)
Cologne (964,000)
Frankfurt-am-Main (651,000)
Essen (616,000)
Official language: German
Religions: Christianity (Lutheran 41%, Roman Catholic 34%), Islam 2%
Government: Federal republic
Currency: Mark, Euro

Storks can often be seen perching on nests on chimney pots. Birds and other wildlife in Germany have suffered from pollution, including acid rain, which has damaged the country's forests.

Printing The invention of movable type in the mid-15th century by the German Johannes Gutenberg speeded up book production and enabled education to spread. The Gutenberg Bible was the first Bible produced by movable type.

Brandenburg Gate This monument, built in 1791, became a symbol of a divided Europe. It stood close to the wall that the communist East German government built to prevent unauthorized crossings to the West. When the wall came down in 1989, Germans gathered at the gate to celebrate.

NORTH SEA

Flen

Bremerhaven

Ham

Oldenburg

Breme

Osnabrück

Ha

Münster

Bielefeld

Dortmund

Duisburg

Essen

Düsseldorf

Wuppertal

Mönchengladbach

Kas

Cologne

Aachen

Bonn

G E R

Koblenz

Eifel

Rhine

Frankfurt-am-M

Mosel

Wiesbaden

Mainz

Darmstadt

Mannheim

Saarbrücken

Karlsruhe

Baden-Baden

Stuttg

Black Forest

Freiburg

Ravensb

Lake Constance

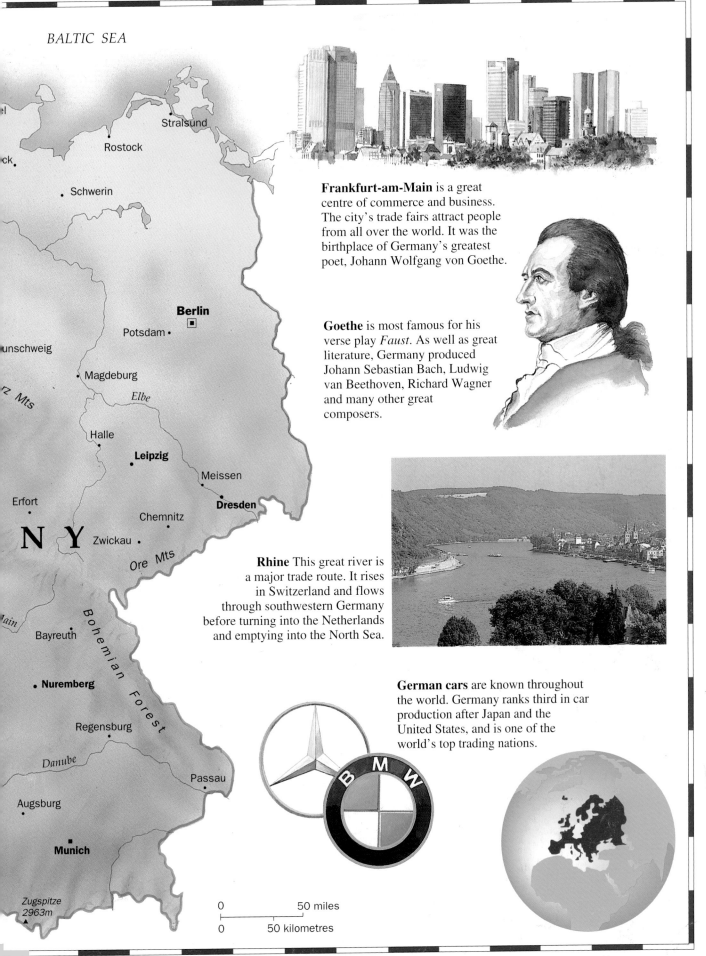

Stralsund
Rostock
Schwerin
ck
el

Frankfurt-am-Main is a great
centre of commerce and business.
The city's trade fairs attract people
from all over the world. It was the
birthplace of Germany's greatest
poet, Johann Wolfgang von Goethe.

Berlin
Potsdam
unschweig
Magdeburg
Elbe
z Mts
Halle
Leipzig
Meissen
Erfort
Dresden
Chemnitz
N Y
Zwickau
Ore Mts

Goethe is most famous for his
verse play *Faust*. As well as great
literature, Germany produced
Johann Sebastian Bach, Ludwig
van Beethoven, Richard Wagner
and many other great
composers.

Rhine This great river is
a major trade route. It rises
in Switzerland and flows
through southwestern Germany
before turning into the Netherlands
and emptying into the North Sea.

ain
Bayreuth
Bohemian Forest
Nuremberg
Regensburg
Danube
Passau
Augsburg

German cars are known throughout
the world. Germany ranks third in car
production after Japan and the
United States, and is one of the
world's top trading nations.

Munich

*Zugspitze
2963m*

0   50 miles
0   50 kilometres

15

MIDDLE EUROPE

Middle Europe consists of Switzerland, Austria and the tiny principality of Liechtenstein, which is sandwiched between them. Western Europe's highest mountain range, the Alps, runs through the region. The magnificent scenery and winter sports draw many tourists to the area. Manufacturing is important and the countries are prosperous. Switzerland is famous for its banks, which have investors from all over the world.

AUSTRIA

Area: 83,859sq km (32,378sq miles)
Highest point: Gross Glockner 3,797m (12,547ft)
Population: 8,072,000
Capital and largest city: Vienna (pop 1,540,000)
Other large cities: Graz (238,000)
Official language: German
Religions: Christianity (Roman Catholic 75%)
Government: Federal republic
Currency: Schilling, Euro

SWITZERLAND

Area: 41,284sq km (15,940sq miles)
Highest point: Dufourspitze of Monte Rosa 4,634m (15,203ft)
Population: 7,088,000
Capital: Bern (pop 134,000)
Largest cities: Zurich (344,000)
Basel (174,000)
Official languages: French, German, Italian
Religions: Christianity (Roman Catholic 46%, Protestant 40%)
Government: Federal republic
Currency: Swiss franc

LIECHTENSTEIN

Area: 160sq km (62sq miles)
Population: 31,000
Capital: Vaduz (pop 5,000)
Official language: German
Religions: Christianity (Roman Catholic 80%)
Government: Monarchy (principality)
Currency: Swiss franc

Watches and precision instruments are famous Swiss products. Switzerland lacks natural resources. Its skilled workers use imported materials to make valuable products.

Alps This magnificent, snow-capped range extends from France, through Switzerland, Austria and northern Italy, into Slovenia. The highest peak in the Alps is Mont Blanc.

Postage stamps provide a useful source of income for Liechtenstein. Many stamps prized by collectors show paintings that belong to the country's prince.

0   100 miles
0   100 kilometres

Pharmaceuticals (chemicals used in medicine) are made in both Austria and Switzerland. Austria produces many luxury goods, such as fine glassware and jewellery, but metals and metal goods are the chief products and exports.

Wolfgang Amadeus Mozart (1756-91) was born in Salzburg, Austria, and started to compose and perform as a child. He was one of the greatest of all musical geniuses. Other great Austrian composers include Joseph Haydn, Franz Schubert and Gustav Mahler.

Edelweiss is a plant with white, star-shaped flowers that grows in the Alps. The upper parts of the Alps are treeless and the vegetation resembles that of the tundra in the Arctic regions of northern Europe.

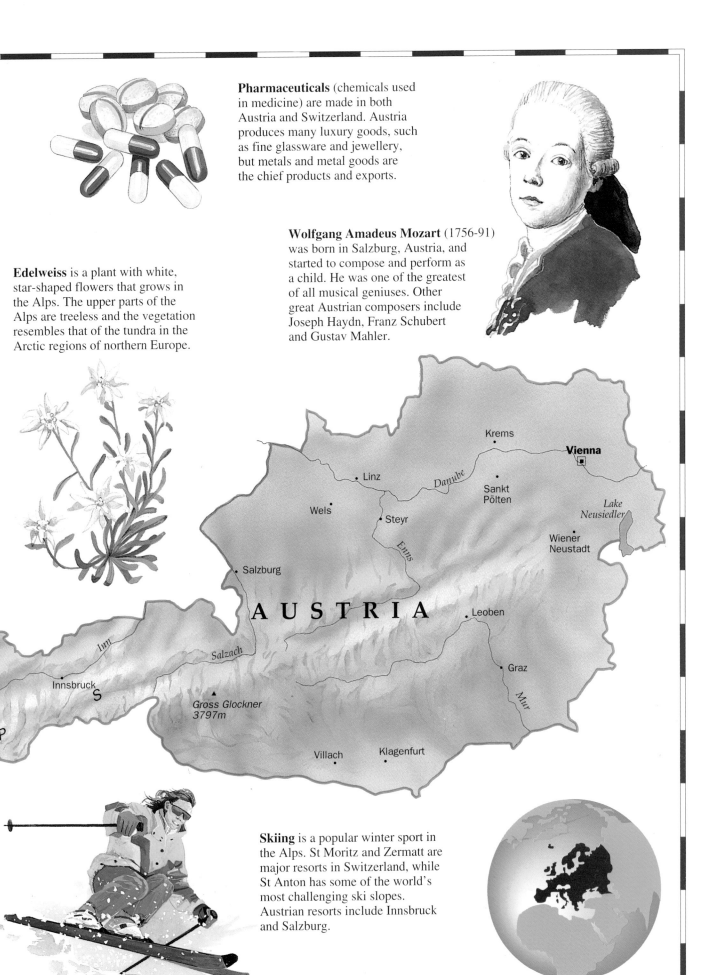

Krems

Vienna

Linz

Danube

Sankt Pölten

Wels

Steyr

Lake Neusiedler

Enns

Wiener Neustadt

Salzburg

A U S T R I A

Leoben

Inn

Salzach

Innsbruck

Gross Glockner 3797m

Graz

Mur

Villach

Klagenfurt

Skiing is a popular winter sport in the Alps. St Moritz and Zermatt are major resorts in Switzerland, while St Anton has some of the world's most challenging ski slopes. Austrian resorts include Innsbruck and Salzburg.

FRANCE

France is the largest country in western Europe. It has a beautiful landscape and fine cities with many historic buildings. It is also one of the world's top manufacturing nations and Paris is a world centre of the fashion industry. Agriculture employs only seven per cent of the population, but France is western Europe's leading producer of farm products. France is famous for its excellent food and wines, and is one of the most prosperous countries in Europe.

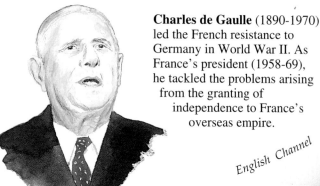

Charles de Gaulle (1890-1970) led the French resistance to Germany in World War II. As France's president (1958-69), he tackled the problems arising from the granting of independence to France's overseas empire.

FRANCE

Area: 551,500sq km (212,935sq miles)
Highest point: Mont Blanc 4,807m (15,771ft)
Population: 58,607,000
Capital and largest city: Paris (pop 9,060,000 including suburbs)
Other large cities: Lyon (1,262,000)
Marseille (1,231,000)
Bordeaux (685,000)
Toulouse (608,000)
Nantes (492,000)
Nice (457,000)
Strasbourg (338,000)
Official language: French
Religions: Christianity (Roman Catholic 76%), Islam 5.5%
Government: Republic
Currency: French franc, Euro

MONACO

Area: 1.5sq km (0.6sq miles)
Population: 32,000
Capital: Monaco
Official language: French
Religions: Christianity (officially Roman Catholic)
Government: Monarchy under French protection
Currency: French franc

Eiffel Tower This wrought-iron tower in Paris is the city's most famous landmark. It was built for the World Fair of 1889. Paris is a great centre of the arts and education, and also a major industrial city.

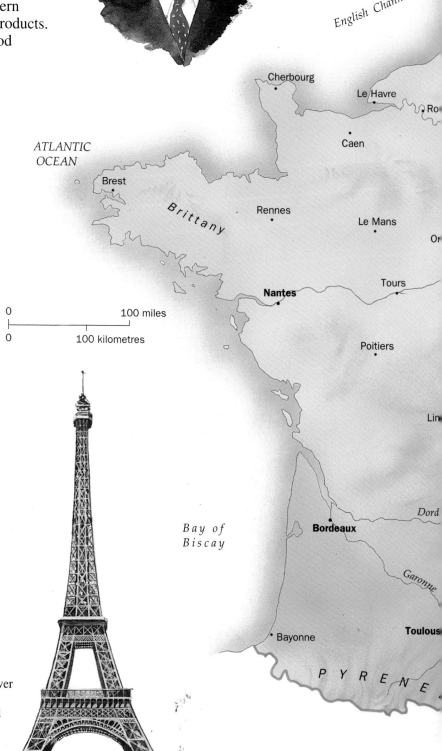

English Channel

Cherbourg

Le Havre

Ro

ATLANTIC OCEAN

Caen

Brest

Brittany

Rennes

Le Mans

Or

Nantes

Tours

0   100 miles

0   100 kilometres

Poitiers

Lin

Bay of Biscay

Dord

Bordeaux

Garonne

Bayonne

Toulous

P Y R E N E

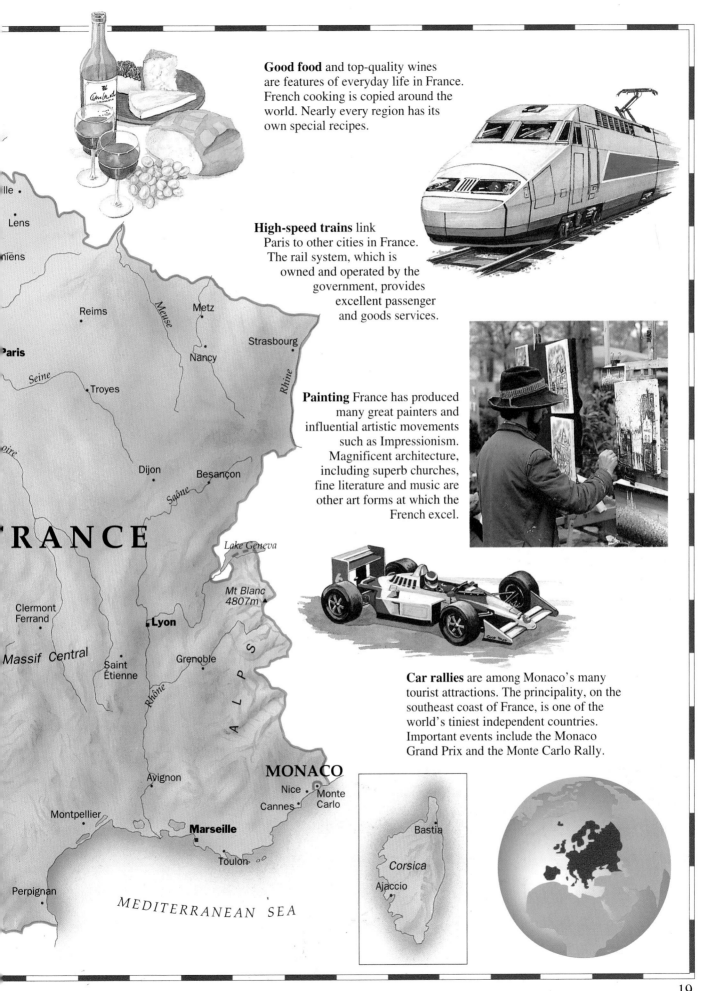

Good food and top-quality wines are features of everyday life in France. French cooking is copied around the world. Nearly every region has its own special recipes.

High-speed trains link Paris to other cities in France. The rail system, which is owned and operated by the government, provides excellent passenger and goods services.

Painting France has produced many great painters and influential artistic movements such as Impressionism. Magnificent architecture, including superb churches, fine literature and music are other art forms at which the French excel.

Car rallies are among Monaco's many tourist attractions. The principality, on the southeast coast of France, is one of the world's tiniest independent countries. Important events include the Monaco Grand Prix and the Monte Carlo Rally.

lle •

Lens

niens

Reims

Metz

Strasbourg

Paris

Nancy

Seine

Troyes

Meuse

Rhine

oire

Dijon

Besançon

Saône

RANCE

Lake Geneva

Mt Blanc
4807m

Clermont
Ferrand

Lyon

Massif Central

Saint
Étienne

Grenoble

A L P S

Rhône

Avignon

MONACO

Montpellier

Nice

Monte
Carlo

Cannes

Marseille

Toulon

Bastia

Corsica

Ajaccio

Perpignan

MEDITERRANEAN SEA

IBERIAN PENINSULA

The Iberian Peninsula consists of two large countries, Spain and Portugal, together with the tiny state of Andorra, in the Pyrenees Mountains in the northeast, and Gibraltar, a small British territory, in the far south. The Canary Islands off the coast of Africa also belong to Spain.

Spain is western Europe's second largest country after France. Spain's economy was shattered by a civil war (1936-39), but since the 1950s it has developed into a fairly prosperous nation. Portugal was a dictatorship from 1933 until 1968. Since 1968, its economy has grown, but it remains one of the poorer members of the European Union.

SPAIN

Area: 505,992sq km (195,365sq miles)
Highest point: Pico de Teide, in the Canary Islands, 3,718m (12,198ft)
Population: 39,323,000
Capital and largest city: Madrid (pop 2,867,000)
Other large cities: Barcelona (1,509,000) Valencia (747,000)
Languages: Castilian Spanish (official), Basque, Catalan, Galician
Religions: Christianity (Roman Catholic 67%)
Government: Monarchy
Currency: Peseta, Euro

PORTUGAL

Area: 91,982sq km (35,514sq miles)
Highest point: Estrela 1,993m (6,539ft)
Population: 9,945,000
Capital and largest city: Lisbon (pop 663,000)
Other large cities: Oporto (302,000)
Official language: Portuguese
Religions: Christianity (Roman Catholic 92%)
Government: Republic
Currency: Escudo, Euro

ANDORRA

Area: 453sq km (175sq miles)
Highest point: Coma Pedrosa 2,946m (9,665ft)
Population: 64,000
Capital: Andorra La Vella (pop 17,000)
Official language: Catalan
Religions: Christianity (Roman Catholic 92%)
Government: Principality
Currency: French franc, Spanish peseta

Bay of Biscay

La Coruña
Gijón
Santa
Oviedo
Santiago de Compostela
Cantabrian Mts
León
Vigo
Orense

ATLANTIC OCEAN

Braga
Valladoli
Oporto *Douro*
Duero
Salamanca
Estrela 1993m ▲
Coimbra
Ma

PORTUGAL
Tajo (Tagus)
Cáceres
S P A I
Guadiana
Lisbon
Setúbal
Badajoz
Evora
Lir
Guada
Huelva
Córdoba
Seville
Lagos
Gra
Sie
Faro
Jerez de la Frontera **Málaga**
Cadiz
Gibraltar (UK)

0 ————— 100 miles
0 ————— 100 kilometres

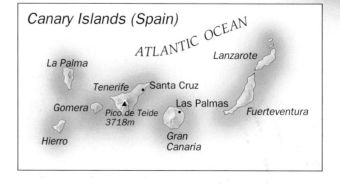

Canary Islands (Spain)

ATLANTIC OCEAN

La Palma
Lanzarote
Tenerife · Santa Cruz
Gomera
Las Palmas
Pico de Teide ▲ 3718m
Fuerteventura
Hierro
Gran Canaria

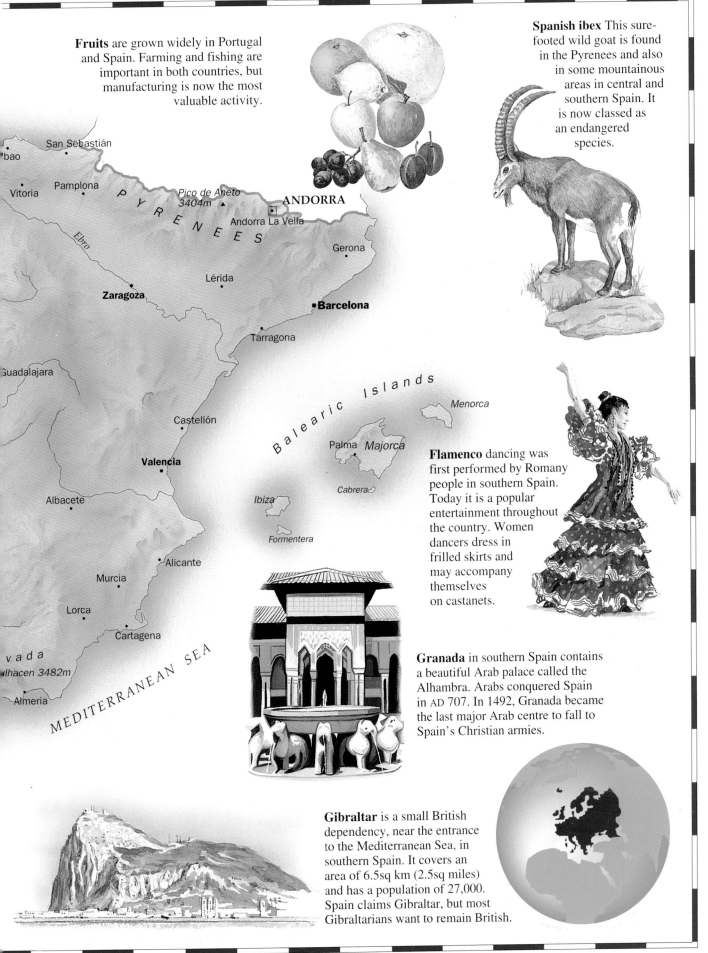

Fruits are grown widely in Portugal and Spain. Farming and fishing are important in both countries, but manufacturing is now the most valuable activity.

Spanish ibex This sure-footed wild goat is found in the Pyrenees and also in some mountainous areas in central and southern Spain. It is now classed as an endangered species.

San Sebastián

bao

Vitoria · Pamplona

PYRENEES

Pico de Aneto 3404m ▲

ANDORRA

Andorra La Vella

Ebro

Gerona

Lérida

Zaragoza

Barcelona

Tárragona

Guadalajara

Balearic Islands

Menorca

Castellón

Palma *Majorca*

Valencia

Cabrera

Albacete

Ibiza

Flamenco dancing was first performed by Romany people in southern Spain. Today it is a popular entertainment throughout the country. Women dancers dress in frilled skirts and may accompany themselves on castanets.

Formentera

Murcia

Alicante

Lorca

Cartagena

vada

lhacen 3482m

MEDITERRANEAN SEA

Almería

Granada in southern Spain contains a beautiful Arab palace called the Alhambra. Arabs conquered Spain in AD 707. In 1492, Granada became the last major Arab centre to fall to Spain's Christian armies.

Gibraltar is a small British dependency, near the entrance to the Mediterranean Sea, in southern Spain. It covers an area of 6.5sq km (2.5sq miles) and has a population of 27,000. Spain claims Gibraltar, but most Gibraltarians want to remain British.

ITALY

Italy extends like a leg and foot into the Mediterranean Sea. The Alps in the far north overlook the fertile River Po basin, where most of Italy's major industrial cities are situated. The 'leg' of Italy contains the Apennine Mountains and, in the southwest, are some active volcanoes, including Etna on the island of Sicily.

   Two tiny independent nations lie inside Italy. They are San Marino and Vatican City, which covers an area about the size of a town park in the city of Rome. South of Sicily is the island nation of Malta.

ITALY

Area: 301,268sq km (116,320sq miles)
Highest point: Mont Blanc 4,807m (15,771ft)
Population: 57,523,000
Capital and largest city: Rome (pop 2,654,000)
Other large cities: Milan (1,306,000)
Naples (1,050,000)
Turin (923,000)
Official language: Italian
Religions: Christianity (Roman Catholic 82%)
Government: Republic
Currency: Lira, Euro

MALTA

Area: 316sq km (122sq miles)
Population: 375,000
Capital: Valletta (pop 9,000)
Official languages: Maltese, English
Religions: Christianity (Roman Catholic 93%)
Government: Republic
Currency: Maltese lira

SAN MARINO

Area: 61sq km (24sq miles)
Population: 26,000
Capital: San Marino (pop 5,000)
Official language: Italian
Religions: Christianity (Roman Catholic 89%)
Government: Republic
Currency: Italian lira

VATICAN CITY

Area: 0.44sq km (0.17sq miles)
Population: 1,000
Government: Papacy
Currency: Italian lira

Rome The Colosseum, a huge amphitheatre dedicated in AD 79, is one of many famous ruins of the Roman Empire. Roman citizens gathered there to watch state-run spectacles, including fights between gladiators and wild animals.

Swiss Guard This body of Swiss soldiers is employed to guard the Pope. Vatican City is the headquarters of the Roman Catholic Church and the Pope is its absolute ruler.

Malta consists of several islands south of Sicily. Valletta, on the largest island, which is also called Malta, is the capital and chief port. Malta became independent from Britain in 1964, though Britain had a naval base there until 1979.

Venice is a city built on about 120 islands in the Adriatic Sea. Its streets are canals lined with beautiful buildings that are increasingly threatened by flooding, pollution and overcrowding by tourists. Italy's cities, historic sites and beautiful beaches attract more than 50 million tourists to the country each year.

Style Elegant fashions and stylish cars are products that have given Italy its worldwide reputation for excellence in design. Around 50 years ago, Italy was mainly a farming country, but it has grown increasingly rich through manufacturing.

Garibaldi (1807-82) Giuseppe Garibaldi was a military hero who fought to unite Italy. In 1860, with the help of 1,000 volunteers known, as *red shirts*, he conquered Sicily.

Pompeii is an ancient Roman town near Naples. In AD 79 it was buried by volcanic ash that erupted from nearby Mount Vesuvius. The volcano has erupted many times since.

Map labels

- Bolzano
- Udine
- Trento
- Treviso
- ona
- Venice
- Trieste
- Padova
- ena
- Bologna
- Ravenna
- San Marino
- Rimini
- SAN MARINO
- rence
- Ancona
- rno
- Perugia
- Assisi
- Tiber
- Pescara
- *Adriatic Sea*
- Rome
- VATICAN CITY
- Foggia
- ITALY
- Bari
- Naples
- *Vesuvius*
- *Pompeii*
- Salerno
- Potenza
- Brindisi
- Taranto
- *Tyrrhenian Sea*
- Catanzaro
- Ustica
- *Lipari Is*
- Palermo
- Messina
- Trapani
- Reggio di Calabria
- *Sicily*
- Etna 3340m
- Catania
- Licata
- Pantelleria
- Valletta
- MALTA

0	100 miles
0	100 kilometres

GREECE AND THE BALKANS

This region in southeastern Europe includes Greece, the centre of a great ancient civilization, Albania, and five countries which, until the early 1990s, made up the Communist country of Yugoslavia. Following the break-up of Yugoslavia, civil wars in Bosnia and Herzegovina, Croatia and in the Kosovo region of the new Yugoslavia have caused great damage and loss of life. The region's land is mostly rugged. Farming is important, but manufacturing is the most valuable activity.

GREECE

Area: 131,957sq km (50,949sq miles)
Population: 10,522,000
Capital: Athens (pop 3,073,000 including suburbs)
Official language: Greek
Religions: Christianity (Eastern Orthodox 94%)
Government: Republic
Currency: Drachma

SLOVENIA

Area: 20,256sq km (7,821sq miles)
Population: 1,986,000
Capital: Ljubljana (pop 270,000)
Official language: Slovene
Religions: Christianity (Roman Catholic 83%)
Government: Republic
Currency: Tolar

CROATIA

Area: 88,117sq km (34,022sq miles)
Population: 4,768,000
Capital: Zagreb (pop 868,000)
Official language: Croatian (Serbo-Croatian)
Religions: Christianity (Roman Catholic 72%, Eastern Orthodox 14%)
Government: Republic
Currency: Kuna

BOSNIA AND HERZEGOVINA

Area: 51,129sq km (19,741sq miles)
Population: 2,346,000
Capital: Sarajevo (pop 360,000)
Official language: Bosnian (Serbo-Croatian)
Religions: Christianity 42%, Islam 40%
Currency: Marka

ALBANIA

Area: 28,748sq km (11,100sq miles)
Population: 3,324,000
Capital: Tirana (pop 243,000)
Official language: Albanian
Religions: Islam 70%, Christianity 17%
Government: Republic
Currency: Lek

MACEDONIA

Area: 25,713sq km (9,928sq miles)
Population: 1,997,000
Capital: Skopje (pop 440,000)
Official language: Macedonian
Religions: Serbian (Macedonian) Orthodox 54%, Islam 30%
Government: Republic
Currency: Denar

YUGOSLAVIA

Area: 102,173sq km (39,449sq miles)
Population: 10,614,000
Capital: Belgrade (pop 1,168,000)
Official language: Serbian (Serbo-Croatian)
Religions: Serbian Orthodox 62%, Islam 19%
Government: Republic
Currency: New dinar

Danube The middle course of this important river forms part of the boundary between Croatia and Yugoslavia. It then flows across northern Yugoslavia. Belgrade stands at a point where the Danube joins the Sava, one of its main tributaries.

Marshal Tito (1892-1980) After World War II, Tito (real name, Josip Broz) served as president of Communist Yugoslavia. He kept the country united. After his death, conflict began between various language and religious groups, which led to a violent break-up of the country.

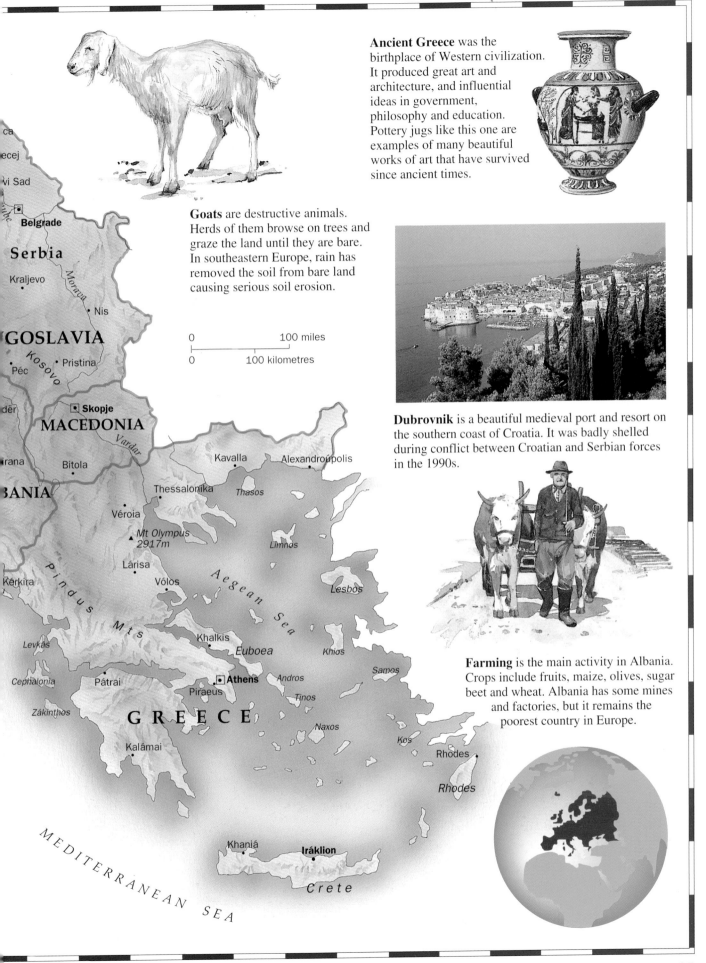

Ancient Greece was the birthplace of Western civilization. It produced great art and architecture, and influential ideas in government, philosophy and education. Pottery jugs like this one are examples of many beautiful works of art that have survived since ancient times.

Goats are destructive animals. Herds of them browse on trees and graze the land until they are bare. In southeastern Europe, rain has removed the soil from bare land causing serious soil erosion.

0   100 miles

0   100 kilometres

Dubrovnik is a beautiful medieval port and resort on the southern coast of Croatia. It was badly shelled during conflict between Croatian and Serbian forces in the 1990s.

Farming is the main activity in Albania. Crops include fruits, maize, olives, sugar beet and wheat. Albania has some mines and factories, but it remains the poorest country in Europe.

ca

ecej

vi Sad

Belgrade

Serbia

Kraljevo

Moraca

Nis

GOSLAVIA

Kosovo

Pristina

Péc

der

Skopje

MACEDONIA

rana

Bitola

Vardar

BANIA

Kavalla

Alexandroúpolis

Thessaloníka

Thasos

Véroia

Mt Olympus
2917m

Limnos

Lárisa

Kérkira

Vólos

Aegean

Pindus

Sea

Levkás

Khalkis

Lesbos

Euboea

Khios

Cephalonia

Pátrai

Samos

Athens

Andros

Piraeus

Tinos

G R E E C E

Zákinthos

Naxos

Kalámai

Kos

Rhodes

Rhodes

M E D I T E R R A N E A N   S E A

Khaniá

Iráklion

C r e t e

EAST-CENTRAL EUROPE

East-central Europe includes Poland, which faces the Baltic Sea. It also includes the landlocked Czech Republic and Slovakia, which until December 31, 1992, formed a single country, Czechoslovakia.

These countries had Communist governments from 1948 until the early 1990s when Communist policies were abandoned. In the 1990s, they faced many problems as they restored the land and government-owned industries to private ownership.

POLAND

Area: 323,250sq km (124,808sq miles)
Highest point: Rysy Peak 2,499m (8,199ft)
Population: 38,650,000
Capital and largest city: Warsaw (pop 1,638,000)
Other, large cities: Lódź (825,000)
Kraków (745,000)
Official language: Polish
Religions: Christianity (Roman Catholic 91%, Orthodox and other 9%)
Government: Republic
Currency: Zloty

CZECH REPUBLIC

Area: 78,864sq km (30,450sq miles)
Highest point: Snezka, in the Sudeten Mountains, 1,602m (5,256ft)
Population: 10,304,000
Capital and largest city: Prague (pop 1,210,000)
Other large cities: Brno (389,000)
Ostrava (325,000)
Official language: Czech
Religions: Christianity (Roman Catholic 39%)
Government: Republic
Currency: Czech koruna

SLOVAKIA

Area: 49,012sq km (18,924sq miles)
Highest point: Gerlachovsky Stit 2,655m (8,711ft)
Population: 5,383,000
Capital and largest city: Bratislava (pop 452,000)
Other large cities: Kosice (241,000)
Presov (93,000)
Official language: Slovak
Religions: Christianity (Roman Catholic 60%)
Government: Republic
Currency: Slovak koruna

Prague, the capital of Czechoslovakia, became the capital of the Czech Republic when Czechoslovakia split apart on January 1, 1993. It is one of the most beautiful cities in eastern Europe.

European bison These animals were once common in Europe, but few now remain. A small herd is protected in the forested Bialowieza National Park which lies partly in Poland and partly in Belarus.

BALTIC SEA

· Koszalin

· Szczecin

• Szczecin

Byd

Pila

Gorzów Wielkopolski

Warta

• Poz

Neisse

Zielona Góra

Wr

Sudeten Mts

Walbrzych

Liberec

Snezka 1602m

Ústí nad Labem

Ore Mts

Elbe

Prague

CZECH REPUBLIC

Plzen

Vltava

Jihlava

Pros

Brno

Ceske Budejovice

Bratis

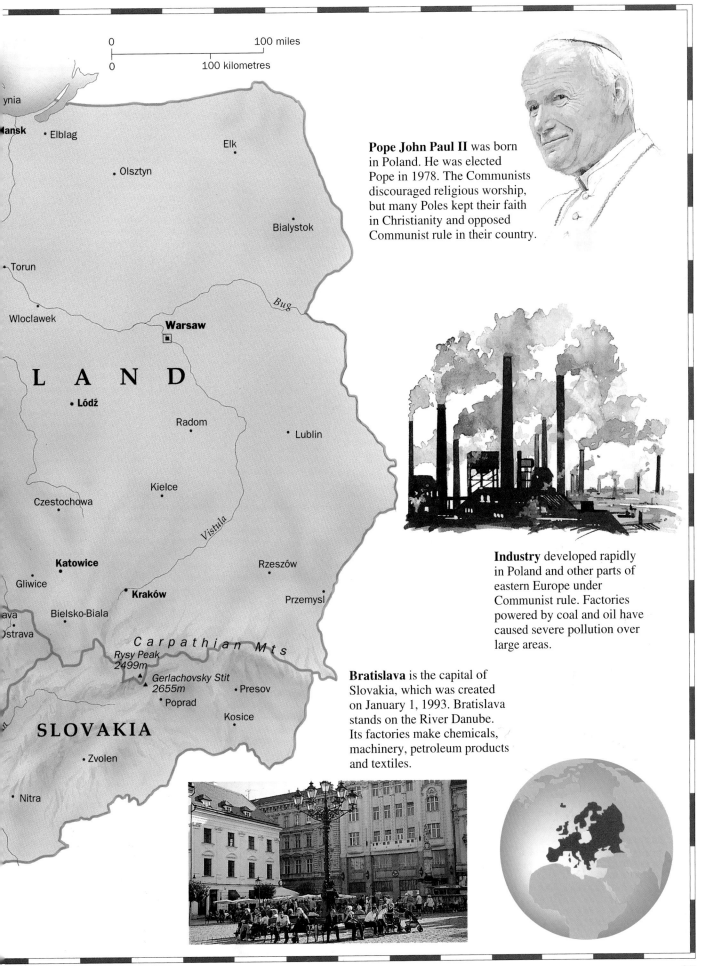

Pope John Paul II was born in Poland. He was elected Pope in 1978. The Communists discouraged religious worship, but many Poles kept their faith in Christianity and opposed Communist rule in their country.

Industry developed rapidly in Poland and other parts of eastern Europe under Communist rule. Factories powered by coal and oil have caused severe pollution over large areas.

Bratislava is the capital of Slovakia, which was created on January 1, 1993. Bratislava stands on the River Danube. Its factories make chemicals, machinery, petroleum products and textiles.

0   100 miles

0   100 kilometres

ynia

Gdansk   • Elblag

          Elk

    • Olsztyn

          Bialystok

• Torun

Wloclawek

        Bug

        Warsaw

L A N D

• **Lódź**

    Radom

        • Lublin

    Kielce

Czestochowa

    Vistula

Katowice

        Rzeszów

Gliwice

  Kraków

        Przemysl

ava   Bielsko-Biala

Ostrava

C a r p a t h i a n   M t s

Rysy Peak
2499m

  Gerlachovsky Stit
  2655m   • Presov
  • Poprad

    Kosice

SLOVAKIA

• Zvolen

• Nitra

SOUTHEASTERN EUROPE

Southeastern Europe contains landlocked Hungary and two countries, Romania and Bulgaria, which have coastlines on the Black Sea. All three countries had mainly agricultural economies until they came under Communist rule in the late 1940s. Today manufacturing is the most valuable activity. In the 1990s, the countries of southeastern Europe faced problems as they worked to restore democracy and private ownership of all economic activity.

 HUNGARY

Area: 93,032sq km (35,920sq miles)
Highest point: Mount Kekes 1,015m (3,330ft)
Population: 10,155,000
Capital and largest city: Budapest (pop 1,885,000)
Other large cities: Debrecen (210,000) Miskolc (178,000)
Official language: Hungarian
Religions: Christianity (Roman Catholic 63%, Protestant 25%)
Government: Republic
Currency: Forint

 ROMANIA

Area: 238,391sq km (92,043sq miles)
Highest point: Mount Moldoveanu 2,543m (8,343ft)
Population: 22,544,000
Capital and largest city: Bucharest (pop 2,080,000)
Other large cities: Constanta (348,000) Iasi (340,000)
Official language: Romanian
Religions: Christianity (Romanian Orthodox 87%)
Government: Republic
Currency: Leu

 BULGARIA

Area: 110,912sq km (42,823sq miles)
Highest point: Musala Peak 2,925m (9,596ft)
Population: 8,312,000
Capital and largest city: Sofia (pop 1,117,000)
Other large cities: Plovdiv (344,000) Varna (301,000)
Official language: Bulgarian
Religions: Christianity (Bulgarian Orthodox 36%) Islam 13%
Government: Republic
Currency: Lev

Wheat is the leading grain crop in southeastern Europe. Maize is also important. Other food crops include fruits, potatoes, sugar beet and various vegetables.

Budapest, the capital of Hungary, stands on the River Danube. Tourists visit the city to see its many historic buildings, but Budapest also has many factories, producing such things as chemical products, textiles and transport equipment.

Wild boars were once common in the forests of central Europe. But most of the original forests have been cut down to make way for farms and cities. Wild boars, along with many other plant and animal species, are now rare.

Dracula, a fictional character, was a vampire who was supposed to have lived in Transylvania, Romania. Legends of vampires may have started because of the many brutal murders committed in the 15th century by Vlad Tepes, a prince who ruled in the region.

0   100 miles

0   100 kilometres

Satu Mare

Baja Mare

Botosani

Dej

Carpathian Mts

Iasi

Cluj-Napoca

Piatra-Neamt

Tirgu Mures

Bacau

ROMANIA

Siret

Prut

Tobacco is grown in southeastern Europe, where it flourishes during the warm and sunny summers. Winters are cold but only severe when icy winds blow from the north.

Sibiu

Hunedoara

Moldoveanu
2543m

Brasov

Transylvanian Alps

Galati

Buzau

Braila

Mouths of the Danube

Ploiesti

Pitesti

Craiova

Olt

Bucharest

Danube

Constanta

Ruse

Dobrich

Mikhaylovgrad

Pleven

Wine is produced in all three countries in southeastern Europe, and Romania ranks among the world's top ten producers. Many of the wines of this region are now exported to western Europe.

Veliko Târnovo

Varna

Balkan Mts

BULGARIA

BLACK
SEA

Sofia

Burgas

Stara Zagora

Musala Peak
2925m

Plovdiv

Blagoevgrad

Roses are grown in Bulgaria to make attar of roses. Only the petals of red roses are used to produce this fragrant oil, which is an ingredient of expensive perfumes. A less fragrant attar is made from a white rose.

EASTERN EUROPE

When the Soviet Union broke up in December 1991, following the collapse of Communism, the 15 republics that comprised the Soviet Union became independent nations. The map of eastern Europe shown here contains six of them. In the 1990s, the governments of the new countries worked to set up new democratic political, legal and economic systems.

Some of these new democratic countries of eastern Europe are now applying for membership of the European Community.

ESTONIA

Area: 45,100sq km (17,413sq miles)
Population: 1,458,000
Capital: Tallinn (pop 435,000)
Official language: Estonian
Religions: Christianity 38%
Government: Republic
Currency: Kroon

LATVIA

Area: 64,600sq km (24,924sq miles)
Population: 2,465,000
Capital: Riga (pop 826,000)
Official language: Latvian
Religions: Christianity 40%
Government: Republic
Currency: Lats

LITHUANIA

Area: 65,200sq km (25,174sq miles)
Population: 3,706,000
Capital: Vilnius (pop 573,000)
Official language: Lithuanian
Religions: Christianity (Roman Catholic 72%)
Government: Republic
Currency: Litas

BELARUS

Area: 207,600sq km (80,155sq miles)
Population: 10,267,000
Capital: Minsk (pop 1,695,000)
Official languages: Belarussian, Russian
Religions: Christianity 49%
Government: Republic
Currency: Belarussian rouble

UKRAINE

Area: 603,700sq km (233,090sq miles)
Population: 59,698,000
Capital: Kiev (pop 2,630,000)
Official language: Ukrainian
Religions: Christianity 43%
Government: Republic
Currency: Hryvna

MOLDOVA

Area: 33,700sq km (13,012sq miles)
Population: 4,312,000
Capital: Chisinau (pop 658,000)
Official language: Romanian
Religions: Christianity (Romanian Orthodox 35%)
Government: Republic
Currency: Moldovan leu

Ukraine has been called the breadbasket of Europe because of the amount of wheat it grows on its vast plains. It also ranks as one of the world's top producers of sugar beet. Wheat is grown throughout eastern Europe.

Amber is the hardened resin of ancient pine trees that grew in northern Europe millions of years ago. A large amount is found along the Baltic Sea coasts of Estonia, Latvia and Lithuania. It is used in jewellery.

100 miles

100 kilometres

Chernobyl, near Kiev in Ukraine, was the site of the worst nuclear accident in history. An explosion at its nuclear power plant in 1986 released radioactive substances into the atmosphere which were carried by winds into northern and western Europe.

Riga is the capital of Latvia. It stands on the Gulf of Riga and has beautiful medieval buildings. It is also a major industrial city, producing chemicals, electronics and machinery.

ebsk

ahilyow

sk

Homyel

rnobyl

■ **Kiev**

U K R A I N E

■ **Kharkov**

Poltava

Luhansk

Kramatorsk

Horlivka

Dneprodzerzinsk

■ **Dnepropetrovsk**

• Makiyivka

Donetsk

Kryvyy Rih

Zaporozje

Mariupol

Kherson   Dnepr

Melitopol

Odessa

Sea of Azov

Simferopol'

Sevastopol

B l a c k

S e a

Wolves, which are one of the ancestors of domestic dogs, are found throughout eastern Europe. They live mostly in open country where there is cover. Their numbers have been greatly reduced by hunting.

Flax is a leading crop in Belarus and Ukraine. These two countries are among the world's top ten producers. Flax fibre is used to make linen, and the seeds to make linseed oil.

EUROPEAN RUSSIA

Only part of Russia, the world's largest country, is in Europe. The rest is in Asia. Russia had a troubled history in the 20th century. In 1917, Communists took power. From 1922, Russia became part of a vast country called the Soviet Union. In World War II (1939-45), German forces invaded European Russia and caused great destruction. In 1991, after Communism had failed to solve the country's problems, the Soviet Union broke up into 15 countries. The largest of these is Russia.

RUSSIA

Area: 17,075.400sq km (6,592,850sq miles), of which about 25% is in Europe
Highest point: Mount Elbrus, in the Caucasus Mountains, 5,642m (18,510ft)
Population: 147,307,000 (about 80% of whom live in European Russia)
Capital and largest city: Moscow (pop 8,400,000)
Other large cities (in European Russia):
St Petersburg (4,200,000)
Nizhny Novgorod (1,400,000)
Samara (1,200,000)
Kazan (1,100,000)
Official language: Russian
Religions: Christianity (Russian Orthodox 16%), Islam 10%
Government: Republic
Currency: Rouble

ASIAN RUSSIA
Asian Russia is thinly populated.
Though three-quarters of Russia is in Asia, it contains only 20 per cent of Russia's people.

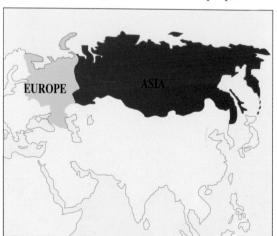

Hammer and sickle
This Communist symbol appeared in yellow on the red flag that was used by the former Soviet Union. It represented the nation's industrial and agricultural workers.

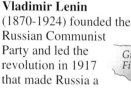

Vladimir Lenin
(1870-1924) founded the Russian Communist Party and led the revolution in 1917 that made Russia a Communist country.

Icons are religious paintings found in Eastern Orthodox churches. The Communists discouraged religious worship, but Christianity survived. The Russian Orthodox Church is the largest religious denomination in Russia.

Murma

Lake Onega

Lake Ladoga

Gulf of Finland

St Petersburg

Chere

Novgorod

Mosc

Kaluga

Smolensk

0	200 miles
0	200 kilometres

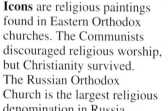

Sea of A

BI

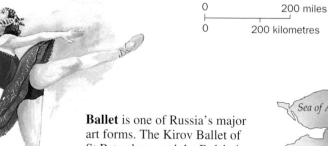

Ballet is one of Russia's major art forms. The Kirov Ballet of St Petersburg and the Bolshoi Theatre Ballet in Moscow are world famous. Russian composers include Nikolai Rimsky-Korsakov, Peter Ilich Tchaikovsky and Igor Stravinsky.

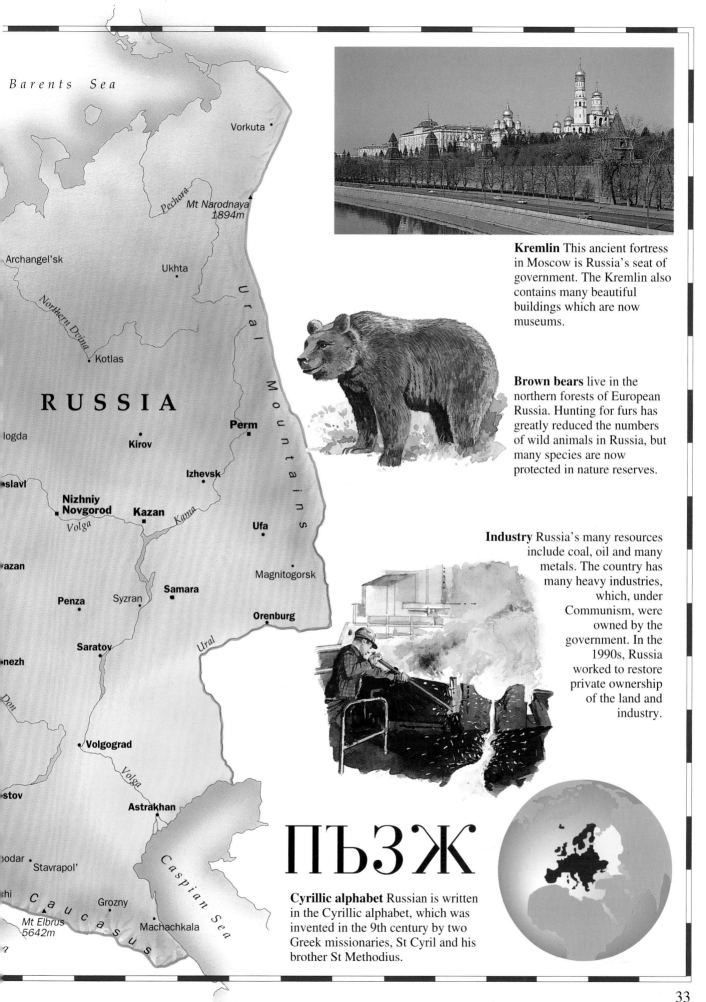

Barents Sea

Vorkuta •

Pechora

Mt Narodnaya
1894m

Archangel'sk

Ukhta

Northern Dvina

• Kotlas

RUSSIA

...logda

Kirov

Perm

Izhevsk

...slavl

Nizhniy Novgorod **Kazan**

Kama

Volga

Ufa

...azan

Magnitogorsk

Samara

Penza Syzran

Ural

Orenburg

Saratov

...nezh

Don

Ural Mountains

• **Volgograd**

Volga

...stov

Astrakhan

...odar •

Stavrapol'

Caspian Sea

...hi

Caucasus

Grozny

▲ Mt Elbrus
5642m

Machachkala

Kremlin This ancient fortress in Moscow is Russia's seat of government. The Kremlin also contains many beautiful buildings which are now museums.

Brown bears live in the northern forests of European Russia. Hunting for furs has greatly reduced the numbers of wild animals in Russia, but many species are now protected in nature reserves.

Industry Russia's many resources include coal, oil and many metals. The country has many heavy industries, which, under Communism, were owned by the government. In the 1990s, Russia worked to restore private ownership of the land and industry.

ПЬЗЖ

Cyrillic alphabet Russian is written in the Cyrillic alphabet, which was invented in the 9th century by two Greek missionaries, St Cyril and his brother St Methodius.

PEOPLE AND BELIEFS

Europe is the home of about 12.5 per cent of the world's population. It ranks third among the continents in population, after Asia and Africa, which overtook it in the late 1990s. Large parts of northern Europe contain few people, but the central plains of Europe and the Mediterranean region contain some of the most densely populated areas in the world. Many people live in huge cities. Europe's largest cities include Paris, Moscow, London, Berlin and Athens.

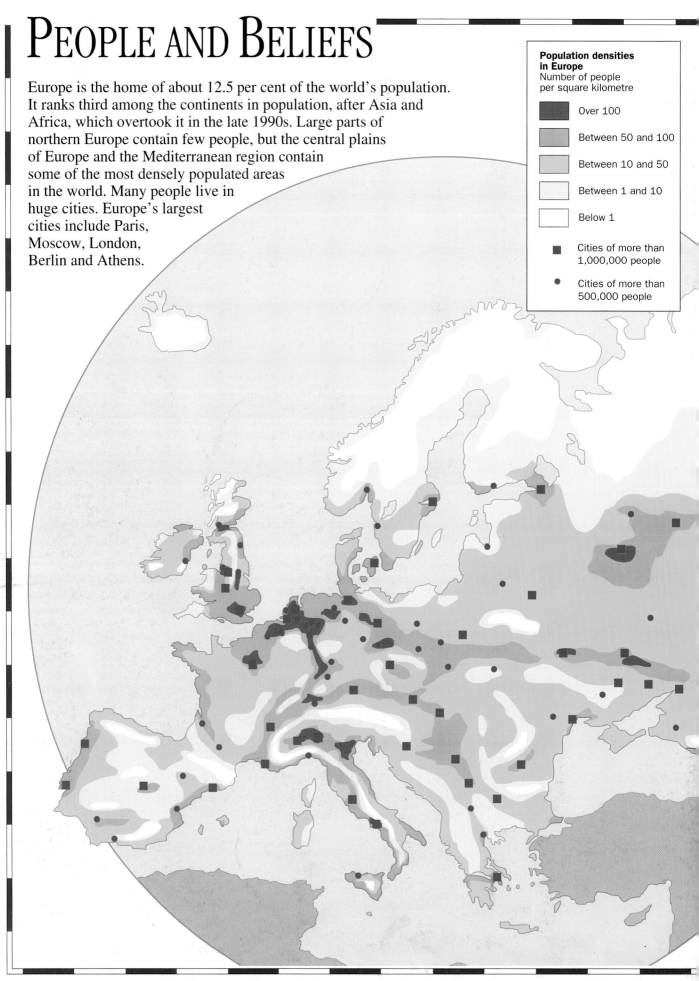

Population densities in Europe
Number of people per square kilometre

- Over 100
- Between 50 and 100
- Between 10 and 50
- Between 1 and 10
- Below 1

- ■ Cities of more than 1,000,000 people
- ● Cities of more than 500,000 people

Population and area

Although only 25 per cent of Russia lies in Europe, it is by far the largest country in Europe both in area and in population. Ukraine, another country created in 1991 when the Soviet Union broke up, is the second largest country, although in population it ranks sixth.

Germany has the second largest population in Europe, although it ranks only sixth in area. The third most populous European country is the much smaller United Kingdom, which ranks eleventh in area.

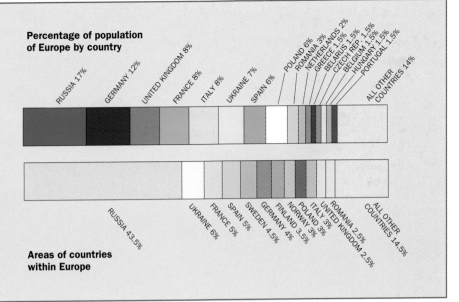

Percentage of population of Europe by country

RUSSIA 17% · GERMANY 12% · UNITED KINGDOM 8% · FRANCE 8% · ITALY 8% · UKRAINE 7% · SPAIN 6% · POLAND 6% · ROMANIA 3% · NETHERLANDS 2% · GREECE 1.5% · BELARUS 1.5% · CZECH REP. 1.5% · BELGIUM 1.5% · HUNGARY 1.5% · PORTUGAL 1.5% · ALL OTHER COUNTRIES 14%

RUSSIA 43.5% · UKRAINE 6% · FRANCE 5% · SPAIN 5% · SWEDEN 4.5% · GERMANY 4% · FINLAND 3.5% · NORWAY 3% · POLAND 3% · ITALY 3% · UNITED KINGDOM 2.5% · ROMANIA 2.5% · ALL OTHER COUNTRIES 14.5%

Areas of countries within Europe

Main religious groups

Christianity, the main religion in Europe, has played an important part in the continent's history, and the great Christian cathedrals testify to its influence on art and architecture.

Roman Catholics make up the largest single group. With their headquarters in Rome, they are strongest in southern Europe and parts of eastern Europe, especially Poland. The other main groups are the Orthodox and the Protestants. Orthodox Christians live chiefly in Greece, the southern nations in eastern Europe and Russia. Protestants live in the northern countries of western Europe. Europe also has Jewish and Islamic communities. Jews live in most parts of Europe, while Muslims live in the Balkans and also in countries, such as France and Germany, that have large numbers of immigrants from North Africa and Southeast Asia.

Under Communism, religious worship was discouraged, but today everyone has freedom of worship. Many people in eastern Europe and elsewhere in Europe do not follow any religion.

Legend:
- Roman Catholic
- Orthodox
- Orthodox and Islamic
- Protestant
- Protestant and Roman Catholic

The great medieval cathedrals of Europe are architectural masterpieces that contain priceless works of art. Thousands of people visit them every year.

CLIMATE AND VEGETATION

Europe's climates range from polar and tundra in the northeast to Mediterranean in the south. The northwest has a mild climate, because temperatures are raised by a warm offshore current, called the North Atlantic Drift – the northern part of the Gulf Stream, which starts in the Gulf of Mexico. Northern Europe has large cold forests of coniferous trees. The natural vegetation of most of central Europe was deciduous forest, with trees that shed their leaves in autumn. Most of this deciduous forest has been cut down to create farmland and space for cities.

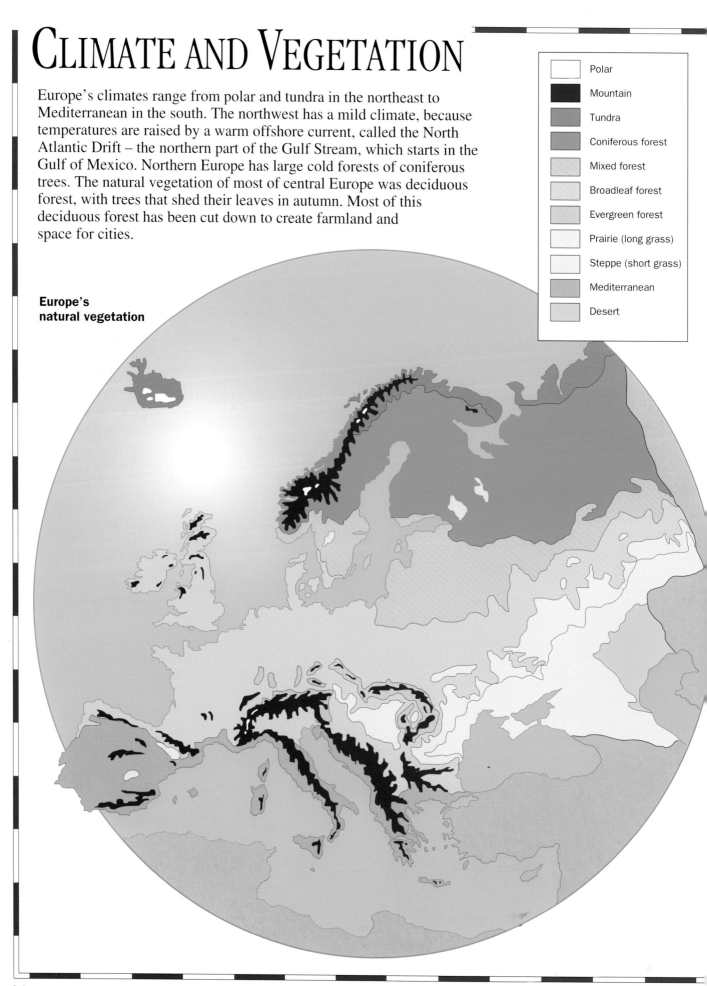

Europe's natural vegetation

	Polar
	Mountain
	Tundra
	Coniferous forest
	Mixed forest
	Broadleaf forest
	Evergreen forest
	Prairie (long grass)
	Steppe (short grass)
	Mediterranean
	Desert

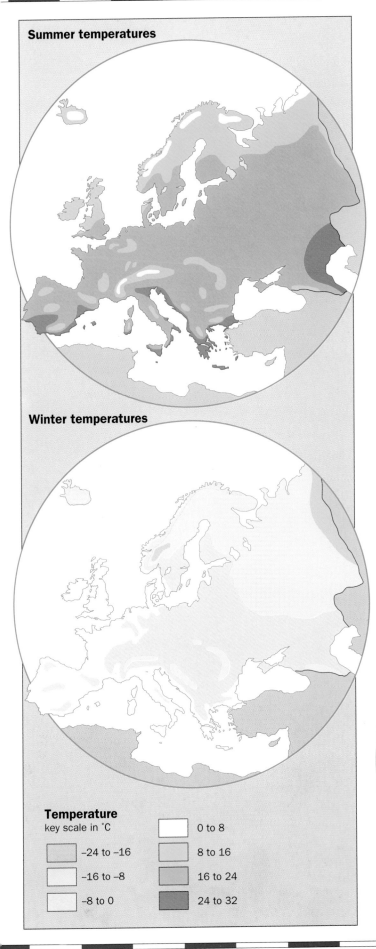

Summer temperatures

Winter temperatures

Temperature
key scale in °C

☐ −24 to −16	☐ 0 to 8
☐ −16 to −8	☐ 8 to 16
☐ −8 to 0	☐ 16 to 24
	☐ 24 to 32

Range of climates

Europe's climate varies from the cold north to the warm temperate south. The climate also changes from west to east. In the west, the climate is influenced by the Atlantic Ocean. The ocean makes summers milder and winters warmer. To the east, the climate becomes more extreme, with hotter summers and bitterly cold winters. Rainfall in eastern Europe is generally less than in the west.

Ranges of vegetation

The three main types of vegetation in Europe are treeless tundra, forests and grasslands. (Mountains, which get colder with altitude, also have these three types of vegetation.) In the coldest northern regions, summers are short. When the topsoil thaws, low plants grow, providing food for herds of reindeer and other animals. The northern forests contain conifer trees that can survive the cold winters. Farther south are mixed forests of evergreen and deciduous trees. Central and southern Europe have broadleaf forests, containing ash, birch, beech, maple and oak. In the Mediterranean, many trees, including pines, cork oaks and olives, have tough leaves that retain moisture during the hot summers and stay on the trees all year. Grasslands occur in regions with dry climates. The best-known grasslands are in Ukraine and southern European Russia. They are called the steppes.

Annual rainfall
in mm

☐ Above 1500
☐ 1000 - 1500
☐ 750 - 1000
☐ 500 - 750
☐ 0 - 500

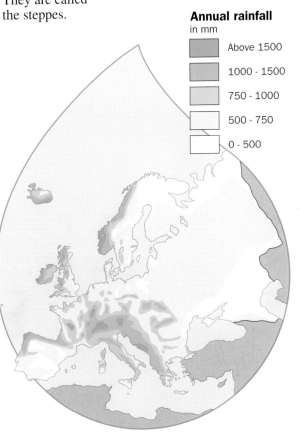

ECOLOGY AND ENVIRONMENT

Europe is a prosperous continent, but economic development has caused great damage to the environment. Farming has destroyed natural habitats, harming wildlife. Industry has also caused pollution – in the air, rivers and seas, and also on land. Pollution from one country often spreads to others. Today, the governments of most European countries are working to prevent further damage.

Seals have suffered greatly in recent years from oil spills and the dumping of toxic wastes.

ICELAND

NORWAY

FINLAND

SWEDEN

ESTONIA

LATVIA

LITHUANIA

KALININGRAD (RUSSIA)

RUSSIA

DENMARK

IRELAND

UNITED KINGDOM

Oil slick

Oil slick

NETHERLANDS

Flood

BELGIUM

LUXEMBOURG

GERMANY

POLAND

BELARUS

Nuclear accident

CZECH REP.

SLOVAKIA

UKRAINE

FRANCE

SWITZERLAND

AUSTRIA

HUNGARY

MOLDOVA

SLOVENIA

CROATIA

ROMANIA

Flood

Flood

BOSNIA & HERZEGOVINA

SPAIN

ANDORRA

YUGOSLAVIA

BULGARIA

PORTUGAL

ITALY

MACEDONIA

ALBANIA

GREECE

Earthquake

Earthquake

MALTA

Environmental damage to land and sea

Area affected by acid rain	▼ Sea dumping sites
Area at risk of desertification	⬤ Worst urban polluters
Most polluted seas	⬤ Major environmental disasters and type
Most polluted rivers	

Natural hazards

Volcanic eruptions occur in southern Italy and Iceland, while earthquakes affect some areas, especially the eastern Mediterranean. Global warming caused by air pollution has begun to change weather patterns. Unusual weather, such as exceptionally heavy rains and storms, has caused severe floods in some areas, such as France.

Damaging the environment

The use of smokeless fuels has greatly reduced air pollution in many European cities, but factories, power stations and motor vehicles still pump poisonous gases into the air. These gases are dissolved by water droplets in the air and return to the ground as acid rain. The chemicals kill trees and wildlife in rivers and lakes. Air pollution has also caused global warming and damage to the ozone layer, which protects us from the sun's harmful ultraviolet radiation.

Intensive farming in dry areas, such as southeastern Spain, has turned once fertile land into barren desert. Industrial and agricultural wastes have polluted rivers, while oil spills from tankers have greatly harmed marine life.

Accidents at nuclear power stations release dangerous nuclear fallout. Europe's worst nuclear accident occurred when explosions and fire damaged a nuclear power plant at Chernobyl, Ukraine, in 1986.

Diseases and deaths

The leading causes of death in western Europe are circulatory diseases, (which cause heart attacks and strokes), cancers and car accidents.

Number of deaths each year from cancer per 100,000 people

| 200 | 225 | 250 | 275 | 300 + |

Number of deaths each year from heart disease per 100,000 people

| 100 | 150 | 200 | 250 | 300 + |

Number of deaths each year from road traffic accidents per 100,000 people

| 10 | 15 | 20 | 25 | 30 + |

Eastern European figures not available

Endangered species

During the Ice Age, a lot of animals became extinct as the ice sheets advanced and retreated. However, since the end of the Ice Age, about 10,000 years ago, the land has been transformed into a patchwork of farms and towns. The destruction of habitats has led to some extinctions, while many animals have disappeared from areas that they once inhabited.

Hunting for food and skins, and the slaughter of animals such as bears and wolves to protect domestic animals, have also reduced the ranges of many creatures. Pressures on wildlife remain as the continuing destruction of hedgerows, land reclamation, military exercises and the growth of tourism continue to reduce natural habitats.

Ladies-slipper orchid

Some endangered species in Europe

Birds and butterflies
Dalmatian pelican
Golden eagle
Swallowtail butterfly

Mammals
European bison
Horseshoe bat
Ibex
Lynx
Otter

Marine mammals
Common seal
Loggerhead turtle

Trees and plants
Bog pimpernel
Dwarf birch
Irish spurge
Ladies-slipper orchid

Economy

Most European countries are highly developed. They produce large amounts of manufactured goods and farm products, but have to import food and many raw materials for their industries. Trade is very important to Europe's economy.

To increase trade and to encourage economic growth, 15 countries – Austria, Belgium, Denmark, Finland, France, Germany, Greece, the Republic of Ireland, Italy, Luxembourg, the Netherlands, Portugal, Spain, Sweden and the United Kingdom belong to the European Union, and 11 of the nations now share a new currency called the Euro. Until the late 1980s, the economies of the Communist countries in eastern Europe were run by their governments. In the 1990s, these countries worked to increase private ownership.

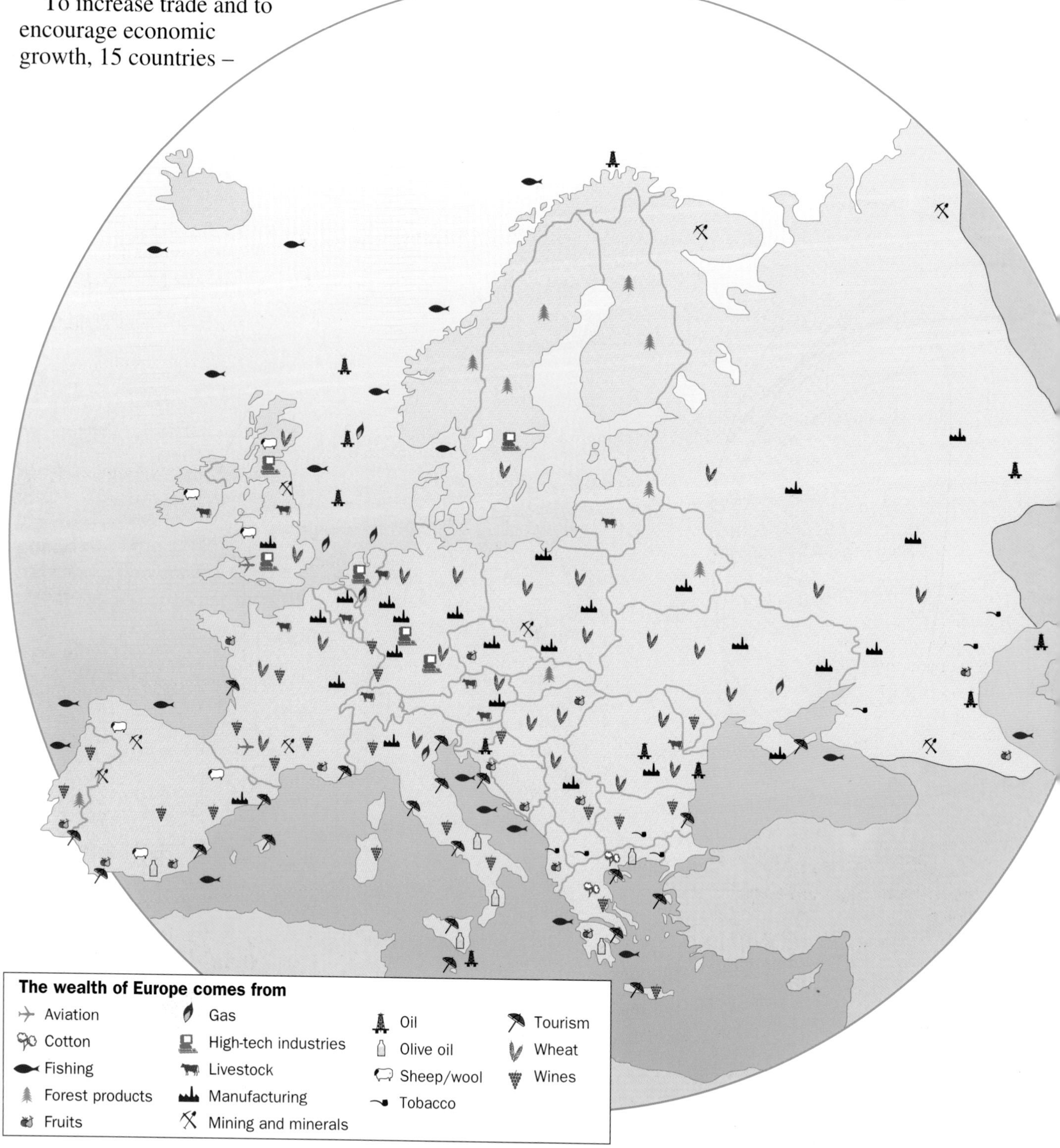

The wealth of Europe comes from
Aviation
Cotton
Fishing
Forest products
Fruits
Gas
High-tech industries
Livestock
Manufacturing
Mining and minerals
Oil
Olive oil
Sheep/wool
Tobacco
Tourism
Wheat
Wines

Gross national product

In order to compare the economies of countries, experts work out the gross national product (GNP) of the countries in United States dollars. The GNP is the total value of the goods and services produced by a country in a year. The chart, right, shows that the countries with the highest GNPs in 1997 were Germany, France, the United Kingdom and Italy. The combined GNP of the 15 members of the European Union is one-tenth larger than that of the United States.

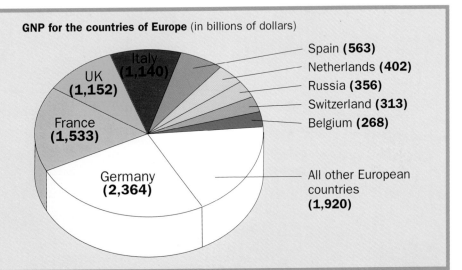

GNP for the countries of Europe (in billions of dollars)

Italy **(1,140)**
UK **(1,152)**
France **(1,533)**
Germany **(2,364)**
Spain **(563)**
Netherlands **(402)**
Russia **(356)**
Switzerland **(313)**
Belgium **(268)**
All other European countries **(1,920)**

Sources of energy

Coal and hydroelectricity were once the chief sources of power in Europe. Major coal producers are Russia, Ukraine and Poland. Hydroelectricity is important in rainy mountainous countries, such as Norway.

Today, oil and natural gas have become major sources of power, while coal has become less important. Europe's oil producers include Britain and Norway, which share the oilfields in the North Sea, and Russia. Leading natural gas producers include Britain, the Netherlands, Norway and Russia. Major nuclear power-producing countries include France, Germany and Russia. Other sources of energy, including tidal, wind and wave power, are now being developed in Europe.

Per capita GNPs

Per capita means per head or per person. Per capita GNPs are worked out by dividing the GNP by the population. For example, the per capita GNP of the oil-rich country of Norway is US $36,100. By contrast, Albania has a per capita GNP of only $760, which places it among the world's poorest countries.

Sources of energy found in Europe

- Oil
- Gas
- Hydroelectricity
- Coal
- Uranium

41

POLITICS AND HISTORY

Between the late 1940s and the 1980s, the democratic countries of the West were opposed to the Communist countries in the east. The tension between the groups was called the Cold War. In the 1980s, the collapse of Communism in the Soviet Union and eastern Europe led to the appearance of new countries on the map. In the 1990s, the West helped the former Communist countries to rebuild their economies. The Cold War was over but new kinds of conflict began. In particular, civil wars occurred when rival language and religious groups fought for power in Chechnya, Russia, and in former Yugoslavia.

The Romans dominated Europe with their army. Foot soldiers regularly marched vast distances carrying equipment weighing more than 40kg (88lb).

Great events

After the end of the Ice Age, around 10,000 years ago, the warm climate led to a rapid growth in the human population of Europe. Around 5,000 years ago, civilizations began to develop in the eastern Mediterranean and, between 500 and 300 BC, the ancient Greek civilization reached its peak. It was succeeded by the Roman empire which developed art, learning and commerce.

Following the fall of the Roman empire, there was a period of decline. The early 14th century, however, saw the beginning of a period, known for its brilliant art and a revival of learning, called the Renaissance. Towards the end of this period in the 15th and 16th centuries, Europeans began to spread around the world.

The Industrial Revolution began in Europe in the late 18th century. In the late 19th century, Europeans colonized much of the world. The 20th century saw two major world wars and frequent changes to the map of Europe. The European empires came to an end, but the century ended with the hope that co-operation between countries could prevent future continental wars.

William the Conqueror defeats the Anglo-Saxons 1066

Irish Potato Famine 1845

Vikings begin raiding western Europe 793

Russian Revolution 1917

Mongols invade from the east 1236

Napoleon defeated at Waterloo 1815

Berlin Wall erected 1961

Spanish Armada defeated 1588

Gutenberg prints first book 1445

Communists take over most of eastern Europe 1948

French Revolution 1789

Reformation begins in Switzerland 1519

Black Death spreads through Europe from southern ports 1346

Visigoths sack Rome AD410 ending the thousand-year empire

Greek civilizations begin 3200 BC

20,000 Evidence of cave dwellers in various sites throughout Europe

6500 Farming in Greece

3200 Early Cycladic civilization in Aegean

1600 Rise of Mycenaean civilization in Greece

1200 Collapse of Mycenaean empire

510 Foundation of Roman Republic

400s Ancient Greece reaches its peak

334 Alexander the Great begins his conquests of eastern Europe, Asia and North Africa

43 Roman invasion of Britain

116 Greatest extent of the Roman empire

410 Visigoths sack Rome

711 Muslim conquest of Spain

793 Viking raids begin

1066 Norman conquest of England

1236 Mongols from Asia attack eastern Europe

1275 Italian explorer Marco Polo reaches China

1290 Spectacles invented in Italy

1337 Hundred Years War between England and France starts

1346 Black Death spre[...] Asia, killing an e[...] 20 million

20,000 BC — AD 1

42

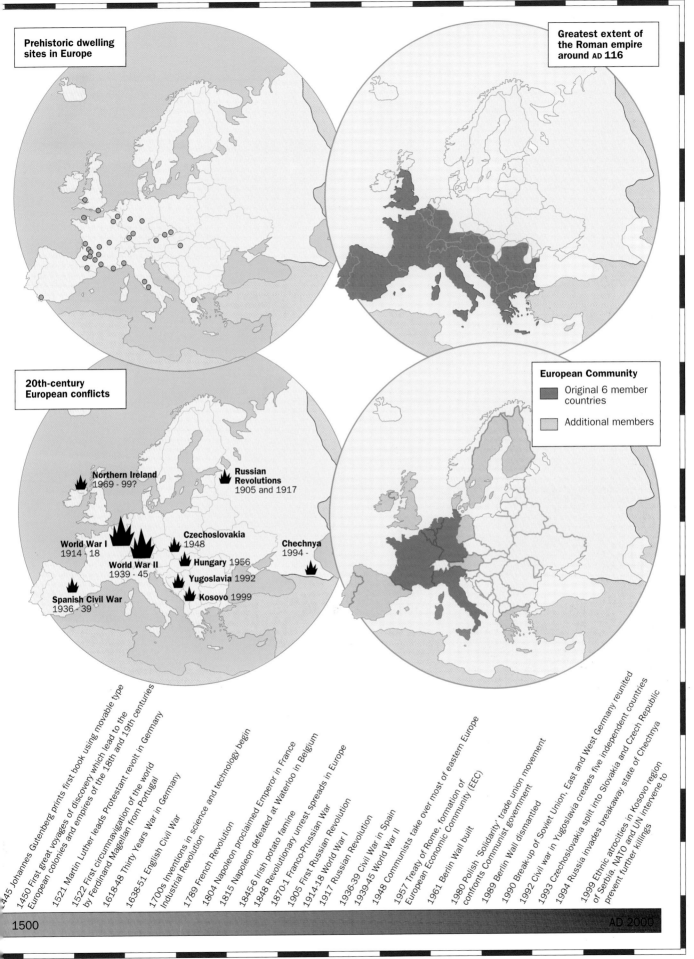

Prehistoric dwelling sites in Europe

Greatest extent of the Roman empire around AD 116

20th-century European conflicts

Northern Ireland
1969 - 99?

Russian Revolutions
1905 and 1917

World War I
1914 - 18

World War II
1939 - 45

Czechoslovakia
1948

Hungary 1956

Yugoslavia 1992

Kosovo 1999

Chechnya
1994 -

Spanish Civil War
1936 - 39

European Community

Original 6 member countries

Additional members

1445 Johannes Gutenberg prints first book using movable type

1450 First great voyages of discovery which lead to the European colonies and empires of the 18th and 19th centuries

1521 Martin Luther leads Protestant revolt in Germany

1522 First circumnavigation of the world by Ferdinand Magellan from Portugal

1618-48 Thirty Years War in Germany

1638-51 English Civil War

1700s Inventions in science and technology begin Industrial Revolution

1789 French Revolution

1804 Napoleon proclaimed Emperor in France

1815 Napoleon defeated at Waterloo in Belgium

1845-6 Irish potato famine

1848 Revolutionary unrest spreads in Europe

1870-1 Franco-Prussian War

1905 First Russian Revolution

1914-18 World War I

1917 Russian Revolution

1936-39 Civil War in Spain

1939-45 World War II

1948 Communists take over most of eastern Europe

1957 Treaty of Rome, formation of European Economic Community (EEC)

1961 Berlin Wall built

1980 Polish 'Solidarity' trade union movement confronts Communist government

1989 Berlin Wall dismantled

1990 Break-up of Soviet Union, East and West Germany reunited

1992 Civil war in Yugoslavia creates five independent countries

1993 Czechoslovakia split into Slovakia and Czech Republic

1994 Russia invades breakaway state of Chechnya

1999 Ethnic atrocities in Kosovo region of Serbia. NATO and UN intervene to prevent further killings

1500

AD 2000

ATLANTIC OCEAN

The Atlantic is the world's second largest ocean after the Pacific. It stretches from the Arctic Ocean around the North Pole to the icy continent of Antarctica around the South Pole. Greenland is the largest of the many islands in the Atlantic Ocean.

Strong currents move through the Atlantic. The warm Gulf Stream starts in the Gulf of Mexico and flows northeast to Europe. It warms coastal areas in northwest Europe. By contrast, the icy Labrador Current flows south from the Arctic and chills the northeastern coasts of North America.

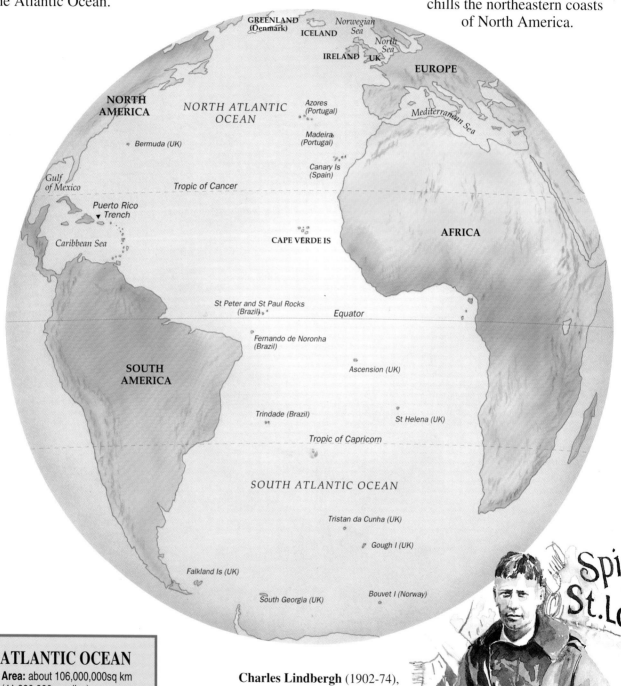

GREENLAND (Denmark)

ICELAND

Norwegian Sea

North Sea

IRELAND UK

EUROPE

NORTH AMERICA

NORTH ATLANTIC OCEAN

Azores (Portugal)

Mediterranean Sea

Bermuda (UK)

Madeira (Portugal)

Gulf of Mexico

Canary Is (Spain)

Tropic of Cancer

Puerto Rico Trench

AFRICA

Caribbean Sea

CAPE VERDE IS

St Peter and St Paul Rocks (Brazil)

Equator

Fernando de Noronha (Brazil)

SOUTH AMERICA

Ascension (UK)

Trindade (Brazil)

St Helena (UK)

Tropic of Capricorn

SOUTH ATLANTIC OCEAN

Tristan da Cunha (UK)

Gough I (UK)

Falkland Is (UK)

Bouvet I (Norway)

South Georgia (UK)

ATLANTIC OCEAN
Area: about 106,000,000sq km (41,000,000sq miles)
Average depth: 3,580m (about 11,700ft)
Deepest point: Milwaukee Deep, in the Puerto Rico Trench, 8,648m (28,374ft)

Charles Lindbergh (1902-74), an American aviator, made the first solo non-stop flight across the Atlantic Ocean in May 1927. Today the ocean is a busy highway and is extremely important in world trade.

Spirit of St. Loui

ARCTIC OCEAN

The Arctic is the smallest of the world's four oceans. It is bordered by North America, Asia and northwestern Europe. It is linked to the Atlantic by the broad Norwegian Sea. The North Pole lies near its centre.

Sea ice covers much of the Arctic Ocean, and this stopped early explorers from finding a sea passage that would be a short cut from Europe to the Far East. They searched for a northeast passage north of Asia and a northwest passage north of North America. The first voyage through the Northeast Passage around Asia took place in 1878-9 and the first through the Northwest Passage was first completed in 1906. Neither route was good for trade.

PACIFIC OCEAN

Bering Sea

60°

Arctic Circle

70°

Permanent pack ice

Beaufort Sea

80°

180°

Laptev Sea

120°

120°

ARCTIC OCEAN

North Pole

Severnaya Zemlya (Russia)

NORTH AMERICA

ASIA

Ellesmere I

Hudson Bay

60°

Kara Sea

Baffin Bay

80°

Franz Josef Land (Russia)

Novaya Zemlya (Russia)

0°

Svalbard (Norway)

Greenland Sea

Barents Sea

GREENLAND (Denmark)

Labrador Sea

Limit of Winter pack ice

Norwegian Sea

ICELAND

ATLANTIC OCEAN

EUROPE

Robert E Peary (1856-1920), a US Navy Commander, was the first explorer to reach the North Pole. He crossed the sea ice with his assistant Matthew Henson and four Inuits, reaching the Pole on April 6, 1909.

ARCTIC OCEAN

Area: about 13,230,000sq km (5,110,000sq miles)
Average depth: 1,120m (about 3,670ft)
Deepest point: about 5,550m (18,044ft) north of Svalbard

INDEX

Numbers in **bold** are map references
Numbers in *italics* are picture references

Picture credits
Photographs: British Airways 11
EEC 4
The Hutchison Library 5, 11, 15, 19, 26, 27, 28, 31
Travel Photo International 5, 6, 12, 23, 25, 33, 35